For the body, mind, &
spirit that infuses
your work

George Kaufm

8/14/19

# Accidental Spirituality

## George Kaufman

### Foreword by Elizabeth Lesser

ISBN 978-1542751049

Published by Scrivana Press,
Eugene, Oregon and Iowa City, Iowa

Design by Niki Harris Graphic Design,
Eugene, Oregon

# Endorsements

George Kaufman's *Accidental Spirituality* is a quilted treasure of spiritual comfort. Where darkness hangs, it illuminates; where confusion reigns, it clarifies; where the heart hurts, it soothes. In this brimming collection of accidental stories, George's courageous zeal for life and commitment to living as a spiritual warrior is as inspiring as it is healing.

> Carla Goldstein, Chief External Affairs officer at the Omega Institute and co-founder of the Omega Women's Leadership Center.

In George Kaufman's brilliant collection, *Accidental Spirituality*, beautifully written essay after essay, we are reminded to slow down and live fully. Kaufman savors the complexity of the human condition. His stories are teachings, sweetly told, filled with wisdom, superbly crafted and consistently entertaining.

> Nancy Slonim Aronie, author of *Writing from the Heart; Tapping the Power of your Inner Voice* (Hyperion) and founder of the Chilmark Writing Workshop on Martha's Vineyard.

I have been the beneficiary of George's wise counsel and friendship for over 25 years. He has an amazing way of distilling life into crystalline truths. *Accidental Spirituality* is a repository of these truths. I have been inspired by them one at a time over these years and it is such a delight to see them all in once place. They will enrich you and make you a better person for the reading.

> David Gershon, CEO Empowerment Institute and author of *Social Change 2.0. A Blueprint for Reinventing Our World*

In his highly personable new book *Accidental Spirituality*, George Kaufman's quiet strength, courage, and gravitas shine through. Each story is an individual gem, a reflection on the human condition and a meditation on living a conscious life. George has lived the spiritual wisdom that he writes about and it is his authenticity that touches and stays with the reader. This is a book that offers calm, clarity, and fortitude for the difficult and complex times that we live in.

> Gail Straub, Co-Founder Empowerment Institute, and author of *Returning to My Mother's House*

# Dedication

To Helen, who has been more than a rock firmly anchored in the ground when I needed stability, and more than the wind behind my back when I needed boldness. This dedication is my chance to honor you for our joint travels in the adventure of life. Without your support I might have been many things—but I wouldn't have been me.

# Table Of Contents

# Foreword

*Accidental Spirituality.* The title for this book is just like its author: funny, self-effacing, thought-provoking, wise. Accidental Spirituality: those two words invite us to open the book's pages without hesitation because we know the author won't moralize or condescend, but at the same time, he will take us into the wide-open and hopeful landscape of the soul. It's a rare person who can be both a fellow traveler on this human journey of accidents, tumbles, and befuddlements, and at the same time, be a trusty guide. This is George Kaufman.

I have known George for many years. We have been colleagues and creative partners on a slew of projects at Omega Institute, the learning center I co-founded in 1977. Back when we started Omega, we had no idea it would become what it is today—one of America's largest adult education and retreat centers. In our early years, we were young idealists following our dreams and interests. As it turned out, those dreams and interests were shared by more and more people as the years went on, and today we welcome 25,000 people every year to our campus programs and even more to our online programs. As Omega grew, so did our need for wise leadership and steady guidance. Enter George.

It usually takes a while to trust the people we work with.

But I trusted George from the moment I met him. And he never did anything to diminish that trust. In fact, as the years went on, I came to value his integrity more than anyone else I've had the pleasure to work with. In his quiet, deliberate, and dignified way, he helped steer Omega through difficult transitions and challenges. He did so with grace and humor and a quality one might not readily associate with a lawyer: *love.* If you gave me only one word to sum up the man, I would say "love." He is love in action.

I've been lucky to have such a colleague. But more than that, I have been oh-so-lucky to have George as a mentor. Several of the chapters in the beautiful book are about mentoring. They are some of the best chapters in the book because George knows what he is talking about when it comes to being a mentor. Omega has a large staff, and George has been a mentor to each and every one of us. In the chapter called Mentoring the Heart, George writes, "The Greeks were among the first to introduce the concept of a wisdom figure who would guide the growth and development of a younger person, a role known as "mentoring." And this is exactly what George did at Omega. He guided the growth and development of us all. It didn't matter if you were younger or older in years, because George was always older in wisdom. If age were measured in wisdom, George would be one of the oldest people on the planet today!

In the pages ahead you will receive so much wisdom, offered to you in bite-size, beautiful, delicious stories.

What a meal you are about to eat! A meal of parables, poetry, quotes, jokes, and spiritual teachings. In one of my favorite sections, George writes about a game of imaginary galactic battles that he plays with his granddaughter, Natalia. At the start of each game, Natalia asks George, "Papa, what's your battle plan?" George's musings about this question sums up the way he interacts with all the people in his life, be they his granddaughter, his friends, or his colleagues:

*"My real battle plan is to love Natalia without limit,"* George writes, *"to be in her world without condition, and to be her ally forever."*

What an honor it has been to have George as an ally all these years. Reading this beautiful book, partaking of his wisdom, and being mentored by his love, you too will gain George Kaufman as an ally forever.

Elizabeth Lesser

# Introduction

I have been involved with the Omega Institute in many capacities for more than 30 years. Its reach has captured my heart and held my attention. For purposes of this introduction, let me simply describe Omega as an holistically oriented educational institution that provides more than 300 programs each year. These programs generally run for a week or a weekend, and are attended annually by some 25,000 participants. The choice of courses is a feast for the curious and a learning opportunity for seekers.

For as long as I can remember, Omega has offered a Thanksgiving luncheon for its staff as a gesture of appreciation for our good fortune. At one of these luncheons, I was invited to offer a blessing before the meal. I felt honored and considered what I might say that would acknowledge the holiday, our staff gathering, and my own beliefs about giving thanks for the bounty we were about to share.

When I look back at the various roles I held at Omega, I realize that the opportunity to offer a blessing at the luncheon was the seed from which *Accidental Spirituality* grew. In the years that followed I continued to offer blessings for conferences and other Omega gatherings. The blessings became more robust, offering more than just blessings—they incorporated stories, ideas, and ways to live in the present moment, notwithstanding the temptation to reminisce about the past or to anticipate the future. I called these blessings reflections.

Each reflection needed to be personally relevant, be molded to some behavior or belief of mine, and be grounded enough for listeners to relate my experiences with their own. Eventually I had gathered quite a number of "blessings," and had begun to think of them as a unified entity of reflective thought that I might share with a greater audience.

Many of the stories are quite personal and intimate. I share them with you as an invitation for you to look at your personal history, your belief systems, and your patterns of behavior. The experiences we share live in our bodies at the cellular level and need to be uncovered, revisited, brought to consciousness and, in the best of all worlds, resolved. Other reflections are lighthearted—intimating that spirituality requires laughter, joy and appreciation as nourishment if it is to thrive.

The *"Accidental"* part of the title is no accident. While writing about everyday occurrences there often emerges the opportunity for a special moment, a time of discovery, that I find new and refreshing. Often, from the most ordinary of circumstances, I have uncovered a spiritual moment. The surprise alone has been enough to take my breath away. When I am aware of this new dimension, the moment is transformative. When my awareness button is disconnected, it is just another moment. I find myself picking over my history and trying to capture all the moments of insight that have come to me. And then I laugh. I have seen one star in a constellation of billions. And I have seen it only briefly.

George Kaufman

# Section 1

# Blessing

Birth is the way biology expresses wonder. From our first cry to our last gasp, we are tied to the ineffable by wonder. What has occurred on this earth billions of times is still fresh at every birth and present at every death. We don't know what causes the first in-breath or the final exhalation. It is a mystery that puzzles us throughout our lives.

Wonder is discovering something the world already knows, but we are learning for the first time. We discover our hands and feet, how to gurgle and make grown-ups laugh. We delight in crawling and the miracle of walking. The brain assimilates a vocabulary and absorbs mathematics. We mistake each activity as a commonplace event. Both our arrogance and our innocence foster the delusion of control. The veil that shrouds wonder becomes thicker as we stumble to control our lives. We blame circumstance for failure and assume talent brings success. In our foolishness we mislabel wonder as structure and structure as value.

What does it take to return life to a state of wonder? It takes an act of surrender. When we are able to surrender, we can thin the veil that separates us from wonder. Surrender is not giving up—it is giving in. As we surrender, we learn again to appreciate the mystery of wonder and marvel at the majesty of life. I welcome wonder as the very young and the very old welcome wonder—with simplicity.

# I Almost Missed the Forsythia

It's early on a Monday morning in April. I am doing my Qi Gong exercises, looking out the picture window at the small forest that my study faces.

I concentrate, breathing in and out in rhythm with my postures, keeping balance, remembering the movements, drifting between focus and instinct, losing, then finding, then losing again, that space where the mind surrenders and movement enters.

I am fifteen minutes into my practice. Suddenly my eyes no longer see an undifferentiated forest of green, yellow, white and brown. There in the center of my vision is a large forsythia bush in full bloom. It has been there all along, and I have been blind to its presence. Outrageous yellow reaching in all directions, tendrils stretching to the rising sun. This early harbinger of spring sings out to be noticed. And I almost missed its song.

Nature is not the only place where our focus can be so narrow that we miss the essence of the experience before us. There is a Good Samaritan training exercise that illustrates how the urgency of time can override intentions and form can trump essence.

In the Good Samaritan exercise, each selected trainee

is instructed to go to the building next door where an audience is waiting to hear the trainee speak on the subject of compassion. Some are told they have plenty of time to reach the building down the block where their lecture will be held. Others are told they are already late and should hurry to reach their destination.

What the trainees are not told is that an actor, disguised as a drunk, has been placed on the sidewalk between the two buildings. Those trainees who were told they had plenty of time stopped, gave comfort to the actor, offered money, and showed a desire to help. Those trainees who were told they were out of time hurried to their destination, ignoring the actor, in order to be on time for their appointment to lecture on the subject of compassion.

Whether we are talking about nature's beauty or the human condition, we are so goal oriented, so acculturated to being on time, that we often miss the nuances that enrich life, deepen experiences, and open new possibilities. We reward punctuality, even when the consequences of punctuality reveal the fragile embrace by which we hold on to our core values.

Of course we want to stop and be helpful. We consider ourselves as compassionate people. Unfortunately, the urge to be punctual overrides our essential nature in favor of short-term goals. It is when our priorities become muddled that we risk stumbling. Only later do we realize the shortsightedness of our decisions and how we have been kept from our goal because our anchor values have been overridden. When that occurs, we need to stop and reorient ourselves, take a deep breath, and slowly exhale. By reframing our experience, we can use the obstacles created by changed circumstances as an opportunity to reinforce our core values.

*What else have I missed?* A smile, a chance encounter, disguised beauty, a cry for help, the silence of friendship, the strength of a partner? As my exercises finish for the morning, I vow to find all the forsythia in my life—the ones I trample down in my haste to move on and the ones that must be cultivated to be seen. I vow to slow down the course of my life so it can be appreciated instead of scanned.

Maybe, just maybe, I am the forsythia bush waiting to be discovered. Perhaps I am the one on the sidewalk needing compassion.

# Compassion

In mid-2015, Helen and I relocated from the East Coast of the United States to Eugene, Oregon. We had been settling in to our new surroundings for almost six months at the time of writing this reflection. Helen is a sculptor, but settling in has taken time away from her productivity. Since arriving in Eugene she has completed only one piece after those six months. Distractions have wormed their way between her talent and its expression. It has been a hard fight to tame the distractions so her talent could shine through, but I believe we have begun. As for me, I had been looking forward to a time when I could write daily, but in relocating, similar distractions have interrupted me too easily and too often. I managed to stumble through one reflection and have been dawdling at the doorway of another. My prior writings are a work product of which I am proud. But I wonder whether they reflect a destination I have reached or a direction towards which I should still be striving.

I know if this had been a relocation of family or friends we would have lots of compassion for the journey they are on. But when we are the subject instead of the observer, life gets complicated. We are not schooled in the arena of self-care, because it shows a vulnerability we would rather hide than examine.

When I think about compassionate action in support of others, I am mindful of actions to be taken and roles to be played: reaching out; listening; being available when needed. Filling these roles can be exhausting, time-consuming, and even unappreciated. We may act compassionately to serve the world or be a difference maker to one individual in a fleeting exchange.

Acts of compassion target things or people outside ourselves. They speak to a generosity of spirit that serves others, and by that service, indirectly helps us. The word *compassion* evokes other words, such as *heart, spirit, love, and soul.* These words often reveal what has sparked the compassion, what has fueled it, and what has motivated our commitment to make compassion an essential element of our lives.

By our generosity of spirit, we create connections between ourselves and those to whom our compassion is directed. However, when compassionate acts also serve to deflect attention from ourselves, we may be using up limited resources without acknowledging our own need for healing. What about generosity of spirit towards ourselves? There are parts of us that need to be nurtured if we want to heal the hurts we carry with us from childhood and those injuries we have suffered as adults in our work, our relationships, our personal ties, and our unmet needs. We guard against their being revealed instead of allowing others to see our unhealed places and to welcome the compassionate acts of others directed to our needs. It requires much more courage to accept compassion directed toward us than it does to focus on delivering compassion to others.

We are missing an opportunity when we give without receiving back. There needs to be a currency exchange, not just an unremitting payout of compassion, by which we are loved not just for what we do, but for who we are. Once we allow compassion to infiltrate our most private layers, we begin to experience the connection between ourselves and the universe, and all the people and pieces that make up our world. When we remove the filter clouding our connectivity and experience the oneness that always exists, we are, in that moment, united and at peace.

What I am describing is simpler to write about than to experience. But a poverty of language is no excuse for avoiding an exploration or deflecting a search. Many years ago, one of my teachers supported me in a search to locate what she labeled as my "concert A." I was ignorant of that term and cautious about revealing to anyone that inner, private part of me where I would be exposed and unprotected.

After a moment's hesitation, I put my faith in her understanding of the exercise I was about to experience. As I lay down in front of her fireplace, she connected her energy with mine, taking my heart to a depth I had never experienced. After passing through what I can only describe as many layers, I reached a state of peace where I felt I could rest forever. There were no distractions. My entire body was in tune with itself and the world. "How you now feel," she offered, "is your concert A, your state of true being. In music, instruments in an orchestra tune to middle A on the piano. You are simply experiencing your concert A."

I have always valued that moment as revelatory. As Boris Pasternak said, "When a great moment knocks on the door of your life, it is often no louder than the beating of your heart, and it is very easy to miss it." The moment of finding my concert A not only revealed to me my true self shorn of defenses, but allowed me to see the connection I had with all living things and their connection to me.

The Bible says that it is more blessed to give than receive. Perhaps so—perhaps not. Either way, I prefer to simply share why I believe receiving compassion is a gift that matters.

The experience of caring for others without taking time to replenish our own energy is exhausting. Unless we find ways to pause from serving others, we may find our capacity to care for ourselves and others deeply diminished. Receiving compassion is a restorative act that can heal the wounds we receive from attending to others and at the same time soothe the places in ourselves that are wounded.

By allowing ourselves to receive compassion from others, we experience the common humanity we all share. We appreciate our similarities rather than emphasize our differences, and understand that we are more alike than unalike.

We hunger for love and friendship. By receiving what is being offered, we establish intimacy and create bonds that enrich our lives. Letting love into our hearts is an affirmation that we matter, that our lives are important, and that we are worthy of the gift being offered.

There is no prescription to be followed, no exercise to carry out. What I have discovered about my own life are the values important to me, when I feel fully alive, and when I lose my way. I have had lots of practice in falling down and getting up, withdrawing and reengaging. I am at an age when wisdom should outshine energy and balance should trump turmoil. But I still shake with frustration at the number of times the reverse holds true and I need to make mid-course corrections.

I know that I want honest people in my life and that I want to treat them with love and reverence. I want to leave nothing unsaid that could create barriers to those closest to me. I know I want to be loved in return.

I want to be relevant in the lives of others, to build relationships grounded on integrity, to keep learning and make sure that curiosity is a cherished value. And I want to support your efforts to find the values that matter in your own life, even if I do so by cheering from the sidelines or writing this piece meant for you.

When committed, don't stop. When stuck, practice compassion. Be gentle on yourself and patient with others. Helping hands are a rare commodity, even when it is your hands that need to wrap themselves around your own body.

Stay the course, don't withdraw, keep engaged, share love, breathe deeply… and know that smiling is an act of inclusion.

# Clutter

I am living in someone else's home and looking at their collection of "things" scattered about and wondering, with some disdain, why in the world would they want to own "that?" From there, it's just a short leap of imagination to envision someone living in my home, asking the same questions. And for these questions, I have no good answers.

I refer to this collection of tangible things (theirs and mine) as clutter. I realize there are different kinds of clutter, so I label this particular species as *object clutter*. In one sense, object clutter is revealing of places, people, and individual histories. In its unorganized state, each object is a chapter in our life, with the chapters randomly assembled. Even when our chapters are well ordered, object clutter represents the hoarding of more than we need. As an example, our six albums of family photographs dating back twenty years is not clutter, it is memorabilia. The six cameras on the shelf next to the albums however, are clutter.

I look at clutter as an act of masking who we are inside a sea of who we were. We not only hide our essence from others by our collection of things, we also hide our essence from ourselves. If that were the only form of clutter in our lives, we might question what harm it causes. The difficulty with object clutter is that it becomes a habit from which other kinds of clutter develop.

The second form of clutter is *mind clutter*. Deepak Chopra once observed that the mind engages in about 65,000 separate thoughts a day. He considered that good news offset by the fact that 50,000 of those thoughts are the same ones we experienced the day before. In meditation we label this inability to quiet our mind as "monkey mind."

When we dart from thought to thought we lose appreciation for what is happening now. We surrender the present by reliving past events or spinning future realities. We are easily distracted from the experiences before us and attend to the latest thoughts our minds spew out.

We need to develop a presence portal, a channel for living in the here and now that is not blocked, not distracted, not overwhelmed, and not hostage to other thoughts. The presence portal is a direction and not a destination. It opens directly to mind clutter and avoids what is unnecessary in favor of what is. When skillfully done, we avoid distractions and enable "monkey mind" to evolve into "quiet mind."

The third kind of clutter is *heart clutter*. We envision the heart as the organ that stores feelings, generates compassion, embraces love, and expresses tenderness. But the heart also has the capacity to hold tight to old hurts, remembered insults, unresolved anger, and damaged goods. I call this phenomenon heart clutter, the hoarding of past negativity that we can't or won't release.

In its extreme form, heart clutter overwhelms our current feelings, leaving us with a memory bank that lacks love. To find our way through this labyrinth of stored emotions, we need to be discerning and practice the art of valuing who we are over the ghost of who we have been.

When we open our hearts, not only are we letting in our capacity to feel all the feelings of the moment, we are letting go what we have made peace with, and letting be what we have not resolved. If our heart can learn to live in the present moment, so can we.

# Where are Tomorrow's Leaders?

"Papa, what's your battle plan?" My granddaughter Natalia has asked me that question for the three years we've been having imaginary galactic battles. Her army is mainly Pokemon, popular characters that came to us from Japan. They have strengths and weaknesses, and the capacity to "evolve" and gain in ability and talent. Natalia is also aided by the usual assortment of additional friends: fairies, ponies, and favorite stuffed animals all lined up on the side of goodness and truth.

My army is made up of trolls, gremlins, dragons and the like, all nefarious creatures that are deliciously despicable, untrustworthy, and vulnerable. I respond that I have a million battle plans. My gremlins can invade her home through the electric wires, scoot down the chimney, hide in the ice cubes, or squat inside her toothpaste.

I can freeze her fairies, melt her ponies, blow her over with tornadoes, and put sleeping potion in the water she drinks, all causing dreadful mischief. But, to no avail. For every weapon I devise Natalia has a counter weapon that is stronger, better, faster, and smarter.

The rules are clear. I am to lose. Every time. I engage but do not triumph. I attempt but do not succeed.

My job is to surrender or be destroyed. I don't make it too easy, but above all I don't win. When we are on a common wavelength, joy radiates from Natalia's body. When I have overstepped my role, I am either lovingly reprimanded or scolded. Those are the unspoken ground rules…but they are not my strategy…my real battle plan.

My real battle plan is to love Natalia without limit, to be in her world without condition, and to be her ally forever. I want her to remember my presence, not my words; my deeds, not my promises; my feelings and not my affect. Today she is into buttons and bows. Tomorrow it will be buttons and beaus.

At issue in these battles is more than goodness over evil, grace over mischief, or even girls over boys. We are in the world of make-believe, and that world may be more important to our future than we can ever know. Make-believe leads to magic, and magic sparks imagination. Imagination feeds creativity, and creativity is the source from which all life springs.

Stultify creativity and the wellspring of life dries up. Feed creativity and the world is bathed in light. Perhaps you are thinking it is impossible to change the world from its current trajectory. If that's your concern, perhaps you will find comfort in the conversation between Alice and the nefarious Queen of Hearts. "There's no use trying," said Alice, "one can't believe impossible things." "I daresay you haven't had much practice," said the Queen. "When I was younger, I always did it for half an hour a day. Why, sometimes I've believed as many as six impossible things before breakfast."

We live in a world that believes leaders are forged through qualities like discipline, structure, and will. That has not worked so well so far, so let us posit a world in which leaders are forged through such qualities as love, tenderness, space and freedom. These leaders of tomorrow are today's children and our future. They believe in impossible things and the power of magic. If we cultivate their dreams, we can reap a harvest of hope and a bounty of endless possibilities. Our work is to keep the windows open, the doors ajar, and the pathways clear.

# Worry

The phenomenon of worry has been part of my make-up for much of my life. As I think about what feeds worry inside myself, I wonder if it is a basic tenet of our western culture or a world-wide phenomenon implanted in all beings. Perhaps it doesn't matter. What does matter, for me and I suspect for most of us, is understanding that worry is a constant element of daily life.

I am now well into my seventh decade of life. During that entire time (perhaps with a little break during infancy), worry has been my long time companion. Its face, features, and focus have shifted from one decade to another, as work, family and responsibilities have taken on different faces. Like the hum on a transmission wire, its perceptible thrum lets me know worry is alive and well, and resident in the inner core of my life force.

At its best, worry anticipates events prior to their occurrence and provides us with time to plan strategies that can mitigate adverse consequences. Worry becomes a problem, however, when planning is replaced by obsessive behavior. At that level, we appear to be unwilling, or unable, to limit either its frequency or intensity and put boundaries on the level of intrusion it causes in our lives. The energy we devote to worry and its capacity to influence our lives have the potential to be a juggernaut overriding anything in its path.

Sometimes our worries are small, personal, and specific; sometimes global, generalized, and diffuse. When worry disrupts our daily lives, insinuates itself into our thinking, and interrupts our life energy, we have become prisoner to our thoughts.

In my own life, worry dominated my childhood. I grew up in a household where childhood illnesses were a source of excessive concern that inhibited our activities and unduly influenced family behavior. We worried about symptoms, babied illnesses, and played at life cautiously. Even today my tendency, whether for myself or a household member, is to reach for medical support to rule out, or rule in, what the symptoms of the moment might presage.

What we worry about can be articulated and described. There is also an emotional response to worry that is experienced rather than described, a feeling state we commonly label as anxiety. While worry is often directed at tangible concerns (such as jobs, relationships, illness, etc.), it also includes expressions of fear about global issues (such as natural disasters, geopolitical dangers) over which we have no control and little that we can do to mitigate their effect.

Ongoing anxiety eventually takes a physical toll on the body. It affects our well-being, damages our heart, and limits our mental acumen. When anxiety feels overwhelming, it can override our capacity to experience joy and shrink our engagement with life from its fullest expression into its narrowest existence. We become less than our dreams and soon dismiss our dreams as unobtainable.

Worry is ingrained in us from childhood by authority figures such as parents, siblings, and teachers. As part of our cultural norm we are taught to welcome worry rather than circumscribe its limits. Worry operates at the cellular level and is often present against our intentions and despite our desires. When it pervades our entire being, it can paralyze our ability to think clearly, act decisively, and live joyously.

When author George Leonard was learning Aikido, his instructor Robert Nadau told George he needed to change his attitude when facing an opponent on the mat from an aggressive stance to a welcoming one where he entered into a "common dance" with his opponent. Nadau informed George that he couldn't succeed in his moves and thrusts without a person on whom such moves could be made. George was advised to look at the other person as integral to practicing Aikido, and to tell such person "Welcome. Welcome to my mat."

Are we able to treat our anxiety similarly? Can we convert our anxiety into welcoming the person at the other end of our mat? Are we able to modify our initial instincts so that we learn to "take the hit as a gift?"

There may be ways to address certain worries through

the use of drugs or professional counseling, and that I leave for others to decide. While drugs properly administered can be quite effective, I am aware they can also be invasive and bring with them unwanted consequences. While counseling in skilled hands can be transformative, it does not fully address the role that we can play in changing our own behavior. In short, whatever we can bring to consciousness will help reduce anxiety. In trying to "live" the change we want to incorporate, I recommend that we address worry by including in our daily life some awareness of beauty, creativity, and service. When we take those steps, we are restocking our shelves with food that supports the soul. The buzz of worry still exists, but its vibration can be reduced to a murmur. We have taken affirmative steps to feed our hearts and starve the elements of worry that drain our zest for life.

Read the poetry of Walt Whitman, William Stafford and Antonio Machado; welcome Rumi, laugh out loud, learn to share, pray for love. Practice kindness and generosity. Revere birthdays and blow out candles with gusto. Believe in yourself, and soon there will be a wave of people who believe in you. Believe in others, and together you will find you have created a support system for life.

# Section 2

# Blessing

We live in two worlds:

The world we construct to fit our story, what we see as our perceived world,

and the world whose story we want to embrace, what we see as our potential world.

In our perceived world:

We see hurts our partner has caused us, but not our contribution to their pain;

We see the rebellion of our children, but not our indifference to their needs;

We see the pettiness of others at work, but not our role in its creation.

In our potential world:

We see the virtues of our partner…and our ability to turn those virtues into brilliance;

We see the gift of children…and our capacity to shower them with love;

We see relationships as a dance…and know that we have a choice to heal or to harm;

We see more clearly, speak more thoughtfully, act more consciously, and live more fully;

We see how we can make a difference in the lives of others, even when the only difference we can provide is to hold a hand, offer words of support, or share love.

In our potential world we have the capacity to truly be ourselves…and it is enough for this lifetime.

# The Muse

Waiting for the muse to show up is frustrating business.
I've put out milk and cookies, same kind I gave to Santa
as a kid, but no voice, no harp, no celestial visitation.
Not even a whiff of fire or brimstone. Maybe next time
I'll leave out a manuscript so she can see just how much
help I need.

If I were writing a book with plot, characters, and
storylines, I'd settle for the muse looking over my
shoulder from time to time and whispering suggestions
about stuck places and fast lanes. But I'm talking about
blank pages and empty screens. A black hole, *nada,
gournisht* (a Yiddish word that equates to nothingness
and is both a description and a pronouncement).

On second thought, I'm so frustrated that maybe I don't
need a muse, maybe I need a lottery wizard. I feel as
though I'm back in eighth grade, apparently invisible,
but still hoping that Myrna in seat 4a will give me
a flirtatious smile instead of a body shift that lands
somewhere between contempt and disdain. If Myrna is
my muse I'm screwed forever. I can only hope that my
muse, wherever she is, doesn't carry grudges.

I decided if my writing depended on help from a
muse—I better learn something about their habits—

otherwise I could end up with Hagar the Horrible and find myself devoting my life to writing potboilers.

I bet all my marbles and asked for the top muse, Calliope, whose specialty seems to be epic poetry. Muses aren't all generosity and beneficence. They've got a nasty streak a mile wide. Cross them and you won't even write a nursery rhyme without boils on your tongue.

So I wait. I summon up the image of Poe and wonder if he wrote his poem "The Raven" with divine inspiration, or just some psychedelic drugs. Maybe it was the muse he heard when he wrote

> ...suddenly there came a tapping; as of someone gently rapping, rapping at my chamber door.

> "Tis some visitor" I muttered, "tapping at my chamber door—only this and nothing more."

Now Poe thinks it's his long lost love Lenore, and I want to grab him by the lapels and say, "Listen, Dummy, it's better than Lenore—it's your muse and a muse doesn't make courtesy calls!" But Poe's too wrapped up in his drama to know one knock from another.

Knock on my door, Calliope, and I'm right there with you. I won't miss a heartbeat and I'll give you credit in the dedication page. Nothing glossy or over the top. Just a sedate appreciation to my muse, C. Being an immortal, you've got lots more writers to seduce. Me, I just got this time around.

I've heard whispers from other writers who claim an inside track straight to you. Some of them go all the way back to Homer and some I hear write for *The New Yorker*. I admit it. I'm not a starving writer sacrificing all for my art. If truth be told, I'm a frustrated lawyer who wants more spice in my life than processing tax returns.

So here's the skinny. Sometimes I think I've got so many ideas, I fumble over where to start. Then when I pick one, it feels unworthy. Who'd care to know about a misdirected crate of oranges that I sent to my ex instead of my current honey with a note that said "to the one true Honeybelle." I didn't find out about my screw-up until my ex wrote me and said "Nice try, but you still owe three months in alimony payments." Anyway, I junked the idea even before I had hauled out another one to consider.

I'm still tapping my fingers on the computer waiting for inspiration.

"You do take long shots—don't you?" Right now I'm working on a story based on three fortune cookie messages that I opened last week when I was eating take out from Dim Sum Heavenly Gardens. Right away I thought of you. The messages were:

Talk about what you know...

Write about what you feel...

Savor what you experience...

It didn't make sense to me until I remembered that the secret to unlocking fortune cookie messages is to add the words "in bed" at the end. That didn't work either, so I kept the idea but changed the tag line. I added the words "as a writer." Now I've got something for us to work with.

Here's my end of the deal. I'll be at the computer one hour every day, for a month. I'll take the fortune cookie messages as nudges from you and write about what's really going on in my life, whether anyone but you reads it or not. I'll try and pay attention to what's in front of me and what's inside of me. I'll even work on savoring the bad moments, because they are often more real than good ones. They grip me tighter, they're harder for me to let go, and they hurt for longer.

When I talk about what I know and put it in writing, I have a sense that what opens up is all the stuff that I don't know, and how not knowing is an okay place to land. I've always hidden my weaknesses, but I'm going to try and deal with stress, and failure, and loss, and all the messy parts of life, as though I *own* them, instead of the other way round. King of the junk pile is still King.

And asking about my feelings may be okay for you; you've been doing it for a couple of millennia. Besides, it's easier for women to get in touch with their feelings than guys. Or at least this guy. But a deal's a deal, and all those knotted up, folded away, dark corners of my being will be coughed up in the service of writing. I hope the royalties cover the costs of a shrink.

If it works, thanks for shining a light on me. And if you were somewhere else dripping honey on another writer's words, I guess I could live with the guy that writes fortune cookie messages. He ain't bad. He'll also get a credit in my dedication, although I suspect he'd rather have a tip than a thank you.

# Thinking about You, Calliope

Dear Calliope,

You know I've been struggling for weeks trying to write a piece on mentoring. My trash bag is filled with rejected text. Just two days ago, a glimmer appeared that pointed in the direction my writing needed to go. Don't know where you were during that time, but was disappointed you weren't with me.

I started out wanting to write on the subject of saying goodbye, and meld that language with the concept of mentoring. You might ask how they fit together. The answer is they don't. But then again, you knew that.

At first I focused solely on mentoring, even offered a title *Mentoring from the Heart* and was almost ready to begin. Staring at the title, I was inspired to remove the word "from" and change the meaning of what I wanted to write. Instead of focusing on the mentor's heart, it would focus on the heart of the student. That was your doing, Calliope, and it paid off. I considered us even.

It took a while to spell the story out and talk about types of mentoring. You watched over my shoulder but didn't interfere. I could have used some grassroots support then, but maybe that's not how you work. I did notice a gauzy linen which created a protective tent over my computer and the language captured on the screen. You could have been weighing whether my writing had enough juice to stay, whether I was going to hang in until the piece was finished, and whether you wanted to add your stamp to the work before it was circulated for comment or read to curious audiences.

I now felt the ending of the reflection was in its proper place at the proper time. I had the sense that you had formed the words through me and let me be the scribe setting them out. D.H. Lawrence wrote in a poem:

"Not I, not I, but a great wind that blows through me."

Thank you for being my wind.

Yours in service,

George

P.S. Next time can we plan an outline for a bestseller? We'd be a great team, though I admit you and Homer weren't bad, just dated.

# Mentoring the Heart

The Greeks were among the first to introduce the concept of a wisdom figure who would guide the growth and development of a younger person, a role known as *mentoring*. In Homer's *Odyssey*, Mentor is a friend of Odysseus, who accepts the role of advising Telemachus, son of Odysseus, during his father's long absences and adventures at sea. Mentor, however, is actually the disguise adopted by Athena, goddess of wisdom and war, who supports Odysseus while he is away.

Today, the term *mentoring* has been diluted by its application in commercial contexts and is used by marketers, advertisers, trainers, clubs, organizations, and countless others to serve their particular interests. Unfortunately, such overuse has thinned its meaning and devalued its function.

When I look back at my growing years and first employment, I realize that no one was talking about finding a mentor or serving as a mentee. The environment was one of competition and, in my chosen career as an attorney, associates struggled alone. If someone gave you a hand up, it was informal, subtle, and not discussed.

In the 1960's when I began to practice law, the

environment at law firms fostered a sense of insecurity among associates. Partners made no effort to relieve the uncertainty that permeated the ranks of associates struggling to find their way, or to praise quality work. The notion of engaging a mentor was a foreign concept. Real men didn't need mentors. Instead, they depended on qualities in their control, such as stamina, brain power, nimbleness, and a thick skin (or at least an appearance of one), to survive the work experience.

In my first job as a lawyer, I spent four years at a New York law firm working for the firm's senior corporate partner. Looking back, I recall a blur of late nights, sacrificed weekends, and foreshortened vacations. Loyalty wasn't an option—it was a requirement that overrode any personal or private needs. I was not offended by the imbalance of time imposed by private practice as I stretched my frame to climb up the seniority ladder. I was sad. It took many years for me to understand the choices and sacrifices required to pursue this career path. The rewards were seductive and the costs shrouded from view.

After I left the firm for a less competitive environment, I began to appreciate how my approach to practicing law had been influenced by the partner with whom I worked daily. Without ever uttering a word on the subject, he taught me through his daily interactions with clients impeccable ethics, responsibility for my actions, and how to treat the legal profession as a service industry. In retrospect, I have come to value his mentoring as a way of teaching skills, ethics, and relationships. I had yet to learn that other forms of mentoring existed.

After forty years in practice, I had participated in several sea changes in associate-partner relationships. I shared what I had learned in a book I wrote that the American Bar Association published called *The Lawyer's Guide to Balancing Life and Work*. Through the book and related lectures I was inviting lawyers to reassess their career paths and encouraging them to consider how they could practice law without losing their soul. I began to appreciate that mentorship is more than an intellectual experience that engages the mind. Mentorship can also evolve from personal experience that touches the heart.

Sometimes we feel secure enough to embrace what I call "life mentoring" as an approach to all the interactions we experience with friends, parents, children, and society. When we are uncomfortable revealing ourselves to others, we resist opening our hearts to this more intimate form of coaching. Closing down protects us from exploring the places where we are vulnerable, and we do so because we may not like what we find, even though whatever we find is part of us.

When we close down our self-exploration, we sabotage our capacity for more intimate and honest relationships. This part of us can change. And when it does, far more than cognitive mentoring is affected. There is a vast difference between having a "change of mind" and a "change of heart." The former is a rational decision open to reexamination; the latter is permanent.

There is much that I could say about mentoring, and most of it guesswork and incomplete. Yet I can offer two statements with certainty. First, mentoring is important and significant. It helps us reach our potential and use that potential to advance our relationships with others. As we respond to this opportunity, the "me" of life is subsumed into the larger "we" of life, inviting us to see the points of connectivity between human beings instead of their differences. We begin to grow as compassionate human beings.

Second, no one arrives at where he or she is without help. Along the way, parents, siblings, and friends mentor in their particular ways. Teachers, elders, and wisdom figures who cross our path also leave an indelible mark. The Chinese proverb "When the student is ready, the teacher will appear" suggests that mentoring is a two-way street where there needs to be readiness to help on the mentor's part, and willingness to learn on the student's part.

Looking back reveals the crooked path we followed to today. Along the way there have been teachers who touched us, values we embraced, choices we followed, and crossroad decisions we have made, all as part of the personal cocktail that has encouraged our slow transition from mind to heart. As teacher Steven Levine asked, "Would you rather be the object of somebody's mind or the subject of somebody's heart?"

As you ponder that question, here are some other

thoughts and inquiries about the care and nurturing of the heart:

> How can our hearts be overflowing and yet not spill a drop?
>
> Or contain a lifetime of tears and not be wet?
>
> Or dance without music, be filled without eating, or pray without words?
>
> Ask old people, children, fools, and lovers.
>
> Speak to poets, writers, singers, and those who laugh often.
>
> Ignore those who value success over happiness, desire over compassion, facts over truth, sight over vision.
>
> What shrinks our heart?
>> Avarice, greed, grasping, dissatisfaction.
>
> What swells our heart?
>> Love, compassion, patience, awareness.
>
> What breaks our heart apart?
>> Separation, anger, hurts, grudges.
>
> What holds our heart together?
>> Memories, friends, laughter, tears, and you.

Wherever there is room for personal growth there is room for mentoring. The aspects of mentoring that deal with professional or financial success are aspects

that I leave for others to explore. I want to be a part of
mentoring that attends to who we are and who we want
to be in our relationships with ourselves and with others.
I embrace that kind of mentoring just as the Greeks
valued mentoring—as a sacred endeavor.

# Language

When we want to express ourselves, we have many tools. Words, of course, are what we use to communicate everything from thoughts and ideas to emotions and feelings. Yet our capacity for expression extends far beyond words. For example, we often use body language to augment the tone of our message. Other non-verbal signals serve a similar purpose, such as the clothing we wear, the tone, speed and volume of the words that we use, the physical space we occupy, the intensity of our presence, and the symbols of wealth or status we bear.

As a lawyer, my office was adorned with college and law school diplomas and my desk was cluttered with memorabilia of successful mergers. Paintings on the wall made a statement. A secretary outside my office made a statement. My listing in the partner section of the letterhead made a statement. At first meetings with clients, these trappings were a form of shorthand that embellished our exchange of information. In turn, clients had their own non-spoken language they brought with them.

I realized that I could continue to collect items from my past to keep my history current, or I could discard these mementos as not being relevant to what inspires me today. More and more, I found myself involved in areas that had little to do with being a lawyer. My interests had expanded in different directions and the symbols I used to value were now only interesting relics in the basement of my house, like armor that no longer served the purpose for which it had been designed. When it was time to sell our house, many of those once coveted trappings were discarded and given away.

There are many variations on the theme of the "armor" we wear that can be found in stories, literature, life experiences, and religion. Growing up, our armor served to protect us against the challenges that life brings to us in our youth. As we enter adulthood we find that the armor that served us so well as a child was forged for different battles than the ones we face as adults and can no longer be counted on to keep us safe.

We long for deeper relationships, more honest interchanges, and value-driven friendships. We still need to be safe when we open ourselves up. That safety can only be generated inside ourselves, and is the composite of our experiences, lessons learned, and faith in our resolve. As we move from how we want to be seen to allowing others to see us as we truly are, we are taking an inner journey that encourages us to make a heart connection with the world. In this phase of life, we are less interested in competition and more concerned with values.

Earlier in this book I wrote about Homer. I was fascinated to relearn that his *Odyssey*, an epic tale more than 2,700 years old, addresses the challenge of finding connective tissue as a quest. When Odysseus returns home to Ithaca after ten years of Trojan wars, he is advised by the blind prophet Tiresias to make a peace offering to the God Poseidon, and is instructed to carry an oar on his shoulder and walk inland until he finds inhabitants "who have never heard of the sea, and who do not even mix salt with their food, who know nothing about ships, nor oars that are the wings of ships." When Odysseus meets someone who tells him his oar looks like a winnowing shovel, he will know that he has arrived, and it is time to make appropriate sacrifices.

In this epic tale, Odysseus is traveling to a place where his heroics are unknown, his reputation nonexistent, and the sea has no meaning. His journey is a solitary affair, and he is required to depend on himself for strength and courage. The instructions Odysseus receives, to bury the oar in the ground at the place where the sacrifice will take place, are a way of appeasing Poseidon. Then he is to return home without this symbol of his past.

For Odysseus, like all of us, the journey home is an internal exploration. Past achievements and conquests won't prepare him, or us, for a peaceful old age and gentle death. Wisdom, inquiry, and openness are the tools for this second journey.

The *Odyssey* may be an ancient story, but it addresses in a modern way the transition from external adventures to internal discoveries. The poet David Whyte said that the soul is "the indefinable essence of a person's spirit and being. It can never be touched and yet the merest hint of its absence causes immediate stress." In all our actions we need to live in the soul place of the event and not settle for being an observer. That event may be our work, our families, an adventure we begin or a relationship we end—it is the sweet spot we seek and we must not settle for less.

So long as we work, at least in the form of a typical job, we have a credential that describes who we are. When we retire from work, that credential no longer serves us. We can either cower at the empty pages we need to fill or embrace change as an interior journey we are about to begin. For some of us, the opportunity to explore the world in new ways, to learn new skills, make new connections and repair old ones, can be exhilarating. We have a choice of either retaining the status quo of our emotions or using the wisdom we have acquired over a lifetime to explore questions of the spirit, embrace the mysteries of the soul, and see the heart as the vessel that contains love, courage, strength and will.

One of my favorite teaching stories addresses the choices before us and the consequences that follow. The scene for the story is a village in India where a merchant finally meets the guru about whom he had heard so much. The merchant is bedecked with dazzling jewelry and exquisite clothing, and has a retinue of servants and several vehicles for traveling. The guru has his begging bowl, wears rags for clothing, and uses broken sandals to cover his feet. The merchant is aghast at what he sees and his heart immediately goes out to provide succor to the guru. "What sacrifices you have made to attain enlightenment," he whispers. The guru responds by telling the merchant that the merchant's sacrifices far exceed his own. "I have surrendered the finite for the infinite," says the guru, "but you, my friend, have sacrificed the infinite for the finite."

Few of us are called to practice the spiritual life of a guru, nor are we driven to acquire the wealth or status of the merchant. We are somewhere between the two, holding on with one hand to our history and with the other feeling our way blindly toward the unknown.

Helen and I recently moved West across the country. We had consciously uprooted ourselves from all that was familiar so we could be near one of our daughters. Friends, family, work, geography, and history were now three thousand miles away, leaving a jagged tear in the fabric that had bound us all together. Our friends admired our courage in leaving what we had built over a lifetime in favor of a new lifestyle about which we had little information We noted how often people used the word "courageous" to describe our decision, whether spoken by casual acquaintances or close friends.

Rather than dispute their assessment, we have had to agree. Our move is taking courage beyond our imagining or theirs. Helen and I have each other, and we both have our daughter and her husband, for support and companionship. We would not have undertaken this journey without them. We knew, but discovered again, that the past can be replenished but not replaced. There is a loneliness that emanates from what we have surrendered. We seek to offset the losses and isolation by calls, travel, and email. The communication we have put in place allows us to endure the change we have initiated, but not to mitigate its effects.

We are not complacent. We have dealt with necessities. We have found new doctors to replace those we left behind. We attend the theatre, have joined a synagogue and created a book club, and we have our writing and clay to let us feel the vibrancy of life. It is time for a more contemplative life, but we are still so new at this changeover that inward searching is at best a modest commitment we are protecting from the wind. We are reaching out to strangers and have been rewarded by kindness and openness wherever we have searched. We realize we are not starting over. Neither of us has 70 more years to replicate or build new history, but we are starting to live the experiment and convert it into a way of life that is palatable, endearing, and fulfilling.

*Where is my oar?* I wonder. *Most people who do this kind of traveling are older or younger than I.* Those who are older move—or are moved—by family to institutions that will care for them. Those who are younger move for jobs, for love, for adventure, or perhaps for climate or because of wanderlust. My oar would have streamers at the end, each colorfully displaying an aspect of my history, my friends, and my work.

When I plant my oar in the soil, am I starting over? And then I realize I'm *not* surrendering the oar and I'm *not* starting over. I'm just trading it in. I want to engage in life through gratitude, I want to explore what is yet before me, and I want to experience a life that is filled with laughter and kindness. I don't know if the oar has been an impediment to my transition, but I no longer need it to define myself or govern my decisions. I begin to understand that what I long for is engagement—a desire to explore what is in front of me and to utter the word "Namaste" to the universe of people that cross my path each and every day.

If print could whisper, I would whisper to you the following questions. *Is your oar something you need or can you part with it? If you surrender that oar, what will replace it? And how do you feel about being seen for who you are and not for what you were?*

Namaste.

# The Business of Mentoring

I often tell a story of three friends who make a living in construction, erecting steel beams on high-rise structures. Every day they share lunch on one of the horizontal beams some eighty feet in the air. One day Mike opens his lunch box, examines the contents, and mutters to no one in particular, "A ham sandwich. Every day a ham sandwich. If I have a ham sandwich tomorrow in my lunch pail I'm walking to the end of the beam and jumping."

His friends are silent, frozen with concern for their buddy. At noon the following day, Mike, Daryl, and Erin take their usual seats on the beam. Darryl and Erin flank Mike, watching his every move, as all three settle in for lunch. They watch as he opens his lunch pail, peers inside, closes it up, walks to the end of the beam, and jumps.

A few days later at the wake, Mike's buddies are shaking their heads in disbelief. How could he take his own life over a ham sandwich? Darryl sips a beer, thinks about the past week, and adds with sadness "And you know the worst part about it all? He made his own lunch."

I think of that story often, as time and again I have the knack of getting in my own way, turning simple events into complex ones, reducing the odds of succeeding, and creating paradoxical actions. At other times, peering into the lunchbox allows me to consider a fresh approach, regardless of who had been the chef until now. These decisions may be joyful or painful, but they are borne out of character and resolve.

Timing is important. I watch myself making choices that will transmute relationships that have been part of me for a very long time. I am referring to my long-term relationship with the Omega Institute, and one reason for writing this reflection is to understand my actions rather than to explain them. I have been a part of Omega for more than thirty years, in roles that have included being a volunteer, board member, staff member, and faculty. Omega is now part of my DNA, influencing how I make decisions, frame choices, and adopt behavior. I own a piece of that edifice, just as that edifice owns a piece of me.

For five years I have announced at the start of each year that I am retiring at year-end (pick any year you like). Within that span of time, I kept reducing the number of days I planned to devote to Omega, but like the asymptote I am always approaching but never reaching the horizontal line. Mathematicians say that the curve reaches the line at infinity, and I won't quibble over what year counts as infinity for purposes of my last W-2.

2015 is indeed a different year. With work limited to one day a week and my new residence on the other side of the country, even I can see where my retirement curve meets the horizontal plane. This is the year I need to pry my fingers off the connecting points I share with Omega so that both of us can breathe without restriction. One of the subtleties of forging (or ending) a relationship with Omega is that it works best when you serve the beast instead of allowing the beast to serve you. Being of service trumps being served, and allows Omega to be unfettered as it continues to explore unchartered territory with fresh voices and new ideas.

After thirty years of an enmeshed relationship, it is time to ask myself *how many ham sandwiches are enough*, even when those ham sandwiches are being consumed from an unfinished space eighty feet in the air. I recognize that what feeds us also limits us. We may become weary of always eating the same fare, but there is a hesitancy to try new items (travel, writing, teaching, meditation, and so on) even though they enable us to explore new opportunities. That's a choice, and having announced that 2015 is my last year at Omega, it would be such a waste not to fill the void with new adventures.

We all have structures we cling to. Whether it's a job, an industry, a location, a marriage, or a belief system, we define ourselves by the focus we bring to the pieces that make up our life. Whether we like how our energy is divided or are distressed by that division, we need to acknowledge "what is" before we acknowledge "what could be."

Change is usually incremental, with the size of the steps defined by the individual undergoing the change.

Circumstances influence change. So do factors such as will, serendipity, events, and choice. Sometimes change comes crashing down on us with little forewarning. When that happens, all we can do is retreat to the essence of who we are, and play out the experience from the sturdiest ground on which we can find to stand.

I look back at Omega as a multi-dimensional mentor, and find it fruitful to explore how influential it was in shaping my behavior. Once you start a retrospective of meaningful experiences, beware! All sorts of patterns are embedded within you. The composite that emerges is a series of individual experiences that have blended together over many years to create principles for self-governing.

Over the years I found that Omega had influenced my behavior at work, bringing a certain flexibility to the way that law is practiced, and work had influenced my behavior at Omega, bringing a rigor to the way that Omega ran its "business".

Shortly after I became connected with Omega, I was serving as a founding partner of a small but growing New York City law firm working with associates and trying to mentor them as I had been mentored—by example more than by fiat.

One particular associate and I worked on complex corporate documents for a client of the firm. Michael was industrious and bright. Some thirty years later he was honored as one of the fifty best non-profit attorneys in America. One day Mike called to tell me that he couldn't have done it without my influence and guidance and made a number of personal and gratifying comments. I blushed and stammered, but down deep I was pleased that I was able to help him in his career and that he made a connection between that career and our work together.

Suzanne Osborn, gifted singer-songwriter, wrote a song called "Chain of Life" to honor those who helped blaze the path along which she steps. She sings,

> I'm makin' my shoulders strong
> For the young to stand upon.
>
> Stepping lightly on the backs
> Of those who hold me up.
>
> It's a chain of life unending,
> Ever new and ever bending.
>
> Grateful is the heart
> For the chance to be alive.

No one does it alone. You might take some quiet time and reflect back on those who helped you, maybe even write a letter to them saying thanks. It won't matter whether the person is long dead or still alive because there is no need to send the letter. Some action that serves as an acknowledgement is a good first step. Then reflect on who you mentored and how you mentored individuals in your life. Finally you might consider ways you will continue to make your shoulders strong for the young to stand upon.

# On Writing

To claim that one has writer's block is to acknowledge a level of conceit. It assumes you define yourself as a writer and that there is something stuck in the flow of words that needs to be unstopped. For writers, a block can take many forms, from an unlimited list of errands that must be done before the decks are cleared for writing to a frontal assault, where the writer sits at the computer waiting in discomfort for words to come. For beginning writers, a lack of experience may make the process of writing seem bewildering. When words aren't flowing onto the computer screen, that sense of having nothing worthwhile to say can arise at one extreme from being worn out after years of prolific writing to not knowing how, and where, to start. In either case, a few guidelines I've developed may demystify the process.

I like to assume that if you write you are a writer. If you have published (even self-published) you are an author. If you want to write but haven't been able to self-start the process, let's get some sacred cows out of the way so you can have an easier time getting started.

Writing is a marriage of two notions. The first is the idea itself. The better the idea the greater the potential for the writer to have something to say. If the idea is unworthy, or maudlin, common, baseless, or inauthentic, we may as well acknowledge that strong words don't hide weak ideas. When the idea is novel we come to the second notion in successful writing: that the words we choose serve as our vehicle of expression. By "expression" I am referring to the clarity of the words chosen to sell the idea to the reader, the vividness of description, the cadence of the language chosen, the heat and passion employed, and the conciseness of the words selected.

Over the years I have read many books on the subject of writing by authors like Natalie Goldberg, Nancy Aronie, Annie Lamott, Stephen King, John Gardner, Ursula Le Guin, and David Mamet, to name a few. Some I agree with, and some I don't.

My list includes suggestions from personal experience and how I have incorporated those suggestions into an active process. My recommendation is for you to adopt those action steps that you think will be helpful, reassess after a month or two, and let go of the ones that aren't working.

While my general comments can be applied to any kind of writing, there are special skills that need to be developed when writing fiction. If your preference is to write fiction, some of the writers listed above should be added to your bedtime reading. They will provide suggestions that address character development, voice, plot, and dialogue. The general comments below apply to any form of writing you want to explore.

1. Fight the Grammar Police.

Growing up, we all came across teachers, advisors, bosses, and parents who downgraded what we wrote because it violated proper grammar. Embarrassed, we eventually grew tired of putting out what we wrote for consumption only to receive commentary that we were not writers unless we could master and adopt the rules of grammar. That message eventually became internalized and we assumed that writing was someone else's provenance.

How you overcome that critical voice, which is now your own, is not easy. I don't know for how many years you have worn the "kick-me" sign, but I bet it's enough that the sign itself is yellowed from age and deeply shopworn. You may even have an invisible critic who sits on your shoulder and provides negative feedback on everything you write. I recognize that the discerning critic serves a useful purpose, but not before your first draft is on paper. If you polish each sentence as you would polish a pearl until it shines, you have a much smaller necklace than if you treat each suggestion gently but not obsessively. Ask, insist if you need to, that the critic take a hike over the next few weeks while you buff the rust off your personal writing machine. When finished, you can invite him or her back to provide helpful suggestions, but not to dismiss or denigrate the work and your effort.

## 2. Write from Your Experience.

Charlie Parker, one of the great jazz musicians, said "If you don't live it, it won't come out of your horn." Your experience is unique to you and has a ring of authenticity when you allow the truth of your experience to live inside the words you write. There are also layers of protection we have knitted over many years to hide our vulnerability, small fibs reflected in the words we choose that allow us to dance around our writing instead of plunging directly into the heart of our experience. If we think of vulnerability as a liability we are always hiding some part of ourselves. If we think of vulnerability as a strength, we open the door to writing with power, weaving words together with grace, and creating a product that moves the reader to recognize himself in your words.

Brother Blue was a storyteller and iconic street performer who was active from the 1970s until his passing in 2009. Through the opportunity that scholarships provided, Brother Blue earned a college degree from Harvard, a master's from Yale, and a doctorate from Union. He then applied his educational experiences to the art of storytelling, a role he embraced for some forty years. Helen and I met Blue at his workshop entitled "Storytelling—The Art of Praying Slow." We both thought it would be relaxing and fun to spend a weekend in the world of storytelling. In the first hour of the program we discovered that Blue wasn't just talking about storytelling, he was talking about telling *your own* story—the one buried deep inside us that we hide from the world. He encouraged us to share *that* story, with its pain and embarrassment, and once told, it would free us to move closer to who we were meant to be. I can't say that Blue's program was either relaxing or fun—but I can say that it was simply *the best.*

Making sure that we squeeze life to the fullest is not easy. As we approach something new, it feels like climbing the steps to the ten-meter board and preparing for a dive into the water below. We are bombarded by doubts, insecurity, and different levels of fear. But I believe the alternative, creating slack instead of tension, is worse.

Many years ago I thought about trying out for summer stock to see if that path could hold me in its embrace. I was in my mid-teens and still deeply vulnerable to parental advice. I have often regretted not taking a swing at that ball thrown down the middle of the plate, and though I found other ways to act and perform, they always felt like a pale substitute as I tried to make an activity be an adequate stand-in for an adventure.

3. Create Sacred Space.

If you're serious about writing, you may want to find a spot in your home or apartment that you dedicate to the craft. Keep the space you have chosen separate from the junk that accumulates in all your other rooms. If you don't have the luxury of such a space, take a small spot that you keep sacred, just a reminder that you are starting an adventure, not an activity. The "where" of writing is highly personal. Some like to write in restaurants or coffee shops, on park benches, or while riding public transportation when a block of time is assured. If you are writing outside the home make sure your writing pad does not share space with shopping lists or the never ending "to do" tasks floating in your head. Be armed with your favorite pen or pencils, set a timer in your mind, and start.

If your space inspires a feeling of dedication and purpose, over time that statement becomes a spiritual center, one that you offer as a prayer when you enter and when you leave. Maybe you keep a crystal on the desk or a mug of coffee from your favorite cup. Each one qualifies as a talisman and a reminder that we have something to say. Just as there are no atheists in foxholes, there are no pretenders once you enter the sacred space.

4. Write as a Form of Discovery

Poet C. Day Lewis said that we write to understand, not to be understood. Writing is an act of discovery, allowing us to explore the crevices of the mind where we have stored, ignored, or expunged powerful experiences. Many of the memories most deeply hidden are hangers-on from our childhood that we have covered over and seemingly forgotten. While we often don't remember events from childhood, the experience of those events lives on in the personality we show to the world.

Childhood is not the exclusive domain for difficult

experiences, as each succeeding decade brings about its own challenging times. I want to broaden our vision and remember that many of those difficult experiences contain both positive and negative features. We may need to undertake some creative sleuthing to recall and, in some cases, relive these experiences in order to understand them. Their influence is obvious. But it requires a core honesty to remember the sounds, tastes, and emotions around an experience and value those qualities for bringing a depth to the experience itself.

Here lies your material, exclusively yours, waiting to be uncovered. If the writing is ready to pour out as images and recollections flood in, embrace the opportunity and capture the words as best you can. If you can only see something that is in the distance and out of focus, capture a word, an emotion, an image, and start writing from that spot. The more you delve, the sharper the image will become and the easier it will be for words to flow.

Writing is like exercising a muscle. The more you write, the more you hone your craft. Pathways become familiar, and words, phrases, ideas, and direction seem easier to uncover. A well-known writer was once asked by an acolyte how he could become a better writer. The author suggested that the enquirer write 100,000 words, and show him the last 10,000. Perhaps when we hope that the muse will guide us in our writing, we may discover that the muse responds to effort. The more you show a dedication to the craft, the more the muse is prepared to help you through the knotty parts. It's the same way you get to Carnegie Hall: practice…practice…practice.

I think of this reflection as a starter set, providing an orientation for your writing to follow, but offering limited guidance for the writing itself. I have chosen to pass over detailed exercises, instructions, or advice on how to make your words shimmer and shine. Exercises to facilitate your writing can be picked up by reading many of the authors earlier identified. What I intend to leave with you is an enthusiasm for the larger aspect of the craft: respect, love, admiration, tenacity, commitment, grit, honesty, and perseverance.

Finally, I wish to share with you a quote from Winston Churchill delivered in a lecture at his *alma mater*, Harrow, on October 29, 1941 during the grimmest days of World War II when he advised the youth to whom he was speaking: "Never give in, never give in, never… never… never… never… never."

# Section 3

# Blessing—Evoking Silence

As we enter into silence, I say welcome.

Welcome to the depths to which your adventure will take you.

To the hard edges and rough corners,

To the mellow rides and soft landings,

To the surprises and disappointments

That silence evokes.

We cannot prepare ourselves for the experience of silence—but we can accept what silence brings.

We cannot always structure our quiet time to be peaceful—but we can welcome whatever appears.

We cannot command ourselves to have an empty mind—but we can welcome all that we meet on our way to emptiness.

As you enter into silence, may you be blessed with

The experience of presence,

The joy of silence,

The gift of time,

And the comfort of shared space.

# Little Days, Big Days, and Salad Days

Did you ever consider how time separates days so they appear to have different qualities? Little Days are days with no special meaning or event attached to them. Most of our days are Little Days, and I would like to explore how we spend those days and what value or meaning we give to them. There is an interior aspect to Little Days, something we can use to see how present we are in what we do, what we say, what we feel, or what we yearn for.

Big Days are the days I attach to the ones with momentous events. Examples are the day you were married…or divorced; the day you started college and the day you graduated. Your first job, first love, first loss, first child…these are all examples of Big Days, and we have barely scratched the surface of what is memorable to us.

And then there are Salad Days. These days, according to Shakespeare, refer to a wild and innocent youth. Over time that definition has transformed (or expanded) so that it is now associated with those periods in our life when we are at the top of our game. Advancing, succeeding, being recognized, promoted, or honored, are all examples of what constitute a Salad Day.

Life is filled with all three kinds of days. Perspective provides distinctions as to the value of each. Time provides us with space to examine what we have learned, and the distance to appreciate its value. It is quite natural that we desire to embrace positive experiences and eschew negative ones. The positive ones reinforce the essential nature of who we are and help ground us in our daily life and highlight when we are in tune with our values, our priorities, our sense of well-being.

Negative experiences may be reflected in our distaste for or revulsion at following a path we may have rejected a thousand times, but which still lures us. These experiences leave us feeling untethered, scrambling to regain our equilibrium, and in search of our core being. In an odd way, negative experiences may lead us back to center, if only because we feel so out of alignment.

The pathway to authenticity can appear in many forms, and often shows up when nothing special is happening—on what I have called Little Days.

Recently, I viewed a video of a lecture delivered in 2012 at a conference developed by the Omega Institute for professionals working with veterans. I remember enjoying what the speaker had to say and the artful way he had constructed the lecture.

I felt I was observing something timeless, something beautiful, not because it was perfect (for nothing is) but because it was real, because it came from the heart, because it was addressing the suffering of humanity, and because our work in the world is to embrace our fellow human beings and find ways to incorporate their suffering within the present moment without damage to ourselves.

The speaker, Jon Kabat-Zinn, delivered a talk that contained two gifts. There was the gift of content—well thought out, fluid, direct, compassionate, and intelligent—and the gift of the presence that wrapped itself around his content. No notes, no power-point presentation, no guide, and no props. It was as though the talk was being created in the moment as he chose from thousands of possibilities a filtered and organized set of ideas to share with us. As I listened to his talk for the second time, I became aware of how the audience and speaker were joined together by the message being delivered and the message being received.

When I recall that talk now, I realize that his content will always remain overshadowed by the feeling of presence he created with the audience. Even though the details of his talk have faded with time, I still recall clearly the way he held the space and interacted with the audience.

I don't know whether Jon's lecturing at Omega was a Big Day for Jon or a Little Day. I know for me it was the kind of Little Day I treasure. My interactions went beyond handshakes and hugs. There was an interiority I saw in others and observed in myself.

That kind of interiority requires no words. It is the place

in each of us that touches our authenticity, our essence, and holds as sacred the essence we recognize in others. It is a realm beyond words, though we may hide behind words as we journey both outward and inward. When we are there, our Little Days are rich and beckoning. When we are caught up in the maelstrom of daily living, Little Days lose their connection to the sacred and simply become ways of passing time.

So often I need to be reminded that Little Days contain all the ingredients necessary to experience an authentic life. Reminders come in the form of a lecture, a greeting, a poem that touches me, or a quiet moment shared with loved ones. All I know is there are boundless opportunities to find, and lose, and find again that essence of my being that I long to embrace.

# Dragons—A Worthy Foe

In the 15th century, when cartographers mapped
the world they referenced the parts of the world that
remained unexplored. The title cartographers gave to the
unexplored territory was *Terra Incognita*, or unknown
territory. Occasionally, a phrase would be added to
the map that stated "Here be Dragons," a warning of
danger, a caution that any adventurer entering these
lands had best prepare for immense challenges. I
am interested because any creature that flies at sonic
speed, breathes fire, can scorch the earth, and is almost
impervious to injury, deserves my attention.

Hear the word "dragon" and our mind conjures up
descriptions, imagines smells, anticipates movement, is
blinded by scales, senses footsteps, and is ready to run.
Our first instinct tells us not to provoke the dragon,
don't call attention to yourself, don't engage. Blend into
the landscape, wear muted colors, speak softly, drain
your emotions, be still.

Will it work? Can we possibly escape the dragon by
appeasement, by diminution, by disappearing? And if we
could buy time by shedding who we are, what terrible
price would we have paid for a temporary respite? To
be rid of dragons we must engage. We must find the
source of their nourishment and learn the interior

landscape where the dragons reside so we can seek to destroy or tame this enemy. The tales of St. George and his victory over the dragon have survived for more than four centuries. The dragon symbolizes fear, and a fear that must be addressed directly if we want to experience fulfilling lives.

*Terra Incognita* has disappeared from maps. Apparently there are no unexplored territories on the planet where you can still write the words "Here be Dragons." But there are territories of the mind as yet unexplored where dragons lurk. Every day we need to decide if we will engage or seek appeasement. Every day our survival skills are tested. We don't always know what triggers the dragons or when they will emerge. What we do know is that if we grow smaller they expand. When we engage, they diminish.

Dragons need to be individually engaged. There is no one-size-fits-all remedy. These beasts are individually cast, formed out of the complexities of our birth, our upbringing, and our own DNA.

Here are some examples of engagement from my own family that demonstrate the ingenuity we possess to create the weapons we need. My older daughter, Dana, at the age of eight, was afraid of the dark. One winter she decided to go to camp the following summer. In her own home, she could sleep with the lights on, a luxury that wouldn't be allowed at summer camp. She decided that being able to sleep in the dark was a necessity. Outside her room was a hallway with a light we always left on. Dana began her assault on the darkness dragon by closing her door a few inches a night—a few inches at a time. Each advance darkened her bedroom more. Each advance brought her closer to blackness. After two months she had succeeding in fully shutting the door, and neutralizing her fear of darkness. Dana was ready for camp.

You may ignore the darkness dragon because it doesn't frighten you, or or you may recall your own battles with blackness and understand the fear it can provoke. We don't get to pick our dragons, but the ones we need to battle find their way inside us, latch on to us at a cellular level, and dare us to challenge their power. There is no difference between fear of the dark and fear of the light. The dragon is simply the fear itself, shape shifting into a thousand different forms, and lodging within us at our places of greatest vulnerability.

My daughter Amy had a different approach. She created an ally to help fight her dragons, an imaginary creature that she called Topping Hat, a lithe, smiling figure that was her moral support and her hidden strength when the unfolding of daily events needed someone she could turn to, cry with, and seek out. Topping Hat adopted the shape of a stuffed lion, and while he never spoke words, Amy always understood Topping Hat's message.

After an absence of many years, Topping Hat appeared in one of Amy's dreams. Amy was now in her twenties. In that dream, Amy is trying to build a house but she can't get the walls to stay up. She tells Topping Hat she can't do it. Topping Hat tells her she can, she needs to work at solving the problem, not despairing, and she will persevere. Near the end of the dream the house has been constructed and Amy looks at what she accomplished with a sense of pride and achievement. Topping Hat, still without words, informs Amy that she has the ability within herself to solve any problem, any challenge, that comes her way. *You no longer need me* is the message Topping Hat conveys. *It had only been a problem of confidence—not talent.* As Amy's dream ends, Topping Hat doffs his hat, runs up a beam of sunlight, and disappears into the ether.

Thank you, Dana and Amy, for following your unique paths and showing me your coping skills. Dragons come in many sizes. They are well disguised, possess different energies, and, with remarkable focus, are drawn to our fears. You have dispatched many dragons in your young lives, and possess the inner core you will need to dispatch those that challenge you in the future.

Your paths have led me to consider the dragons in my own life and how I address them. Among the bevy of dragons I am dealing with today, I have been trying to understand my relationship to Parkinson's, a disease with which I was first diagnosed in the winter of 2005. When a name was given to the symptoms I was experiencing, it was hard to appreciate the journey in front of me. The dragon had arrived and taken residence in my body. How it would reflect itself symptomatically would be revealed over time. The tremor became the dragon, the coughing became the dragon, the cold weather that chilled my muscles became the dragon, and even my lack of balance became the dragon.

With each symptom threatening to alter my way of life I realized that the dragon was not without limitations. I could ameliorate these symptoms in both conventional and holistic ways. Drugs, yoga, Qi Gong, exercise, acupuncture, energy medicine. I became a poster child for alternative remedies, trying some, discarding many, selecting a few. I do not believe the Parkinsons' symptoms will disappear. But they can be slowed down, occasionally neutralized, and temporarily thwarted.

Addressing Parkinson's in the way it shows up in my body takes energy and time. But that's not where the dragon lies; that is just a feint the dragon dangles before me to draw my attention away from my coping system. The dragon knows I have contained my fears by constructing a cauldron of love, spirit, tenacity, and direction. It seeks to dismantle the cauldron, pierce the container, and spew the components of fear wherever its unleashed forces choose to wander.

The Parkinson dragon is mine to battle. Someone else battles the cancer dragon, the heart dragon, the dementia dragon, the dragon of hate, or the dragons of obsession or passivity. We cannot rid ourselves of the dragons we face and we don't know where or how they will surface next. We have arrived at the *Terra Incognita* of the mind. Now we can appreciate what is written on the cartographer's maps, and our responses let us know how well we meet the challenges.

I am aging faster than my dragons. I know the range of symptoms I face over time. Fear wants us to image that range immediately. Grace wants to respond only to what is before us. A friend of mine whose livelihood in theatre was threatened by an illness that some day could affect her amazing singing voice was told by her mentor "Don't play the third act in the opening scene!" The awareness that life is to be lived in the present moment, even as we live from moment to moment, is the greatest weapon we own in battling dragons. That message is centuries old and pre-dates dragons. It is simple to understand, complex to initiate, and vital to possess.

# Nothing Happened

I've been wrestling with how to shape this reflection.
At the moment, the thoughts I want to capture feel like
elusive wisps—just a faint glow in the distance toward
which I am stumbling. The desire to write is strong,
but I am waiting for a voice to emerge. Little seems
to bubble to the surface, and what becomes visible
vanishes as it sees the light of day. Perhaps it is a clue
to the roiling below, yet the disturbances are so deeply
submerged that what shows on the surface are only the
bubbles popping and the faint hiss of gas as their shape
dissolves into thin air.

Here's where I need to hold onto the process I teach,
write about, and believe in. Just dive in and eventually
the words will follow. I want to write about days when
nothing happened and challenge the truth of that belief.
Of course a million things happened. Just pick up a
paper and scan the headlines. Walk into an ER at any
hospital and feel the pulse of all that is going on. Google
the births and deaths that occur around the world on
any day. Families, friends, co-workers, doctors, nurses
and orderlies, mid-wives, priests, and funeral directors
all know that many things, often profound things,
have happened. Follow rhythms, catch sounds, observe
emotions, as patterns emerge and you become aware of

life and its teeming energy.

The days where "nothing happens," however, are the ones I'd like to address. I want to describe what happens in a day that I say "nothing happened." Take yesterday, for example. My morning began with T'ai Chi and exercise. Helen joined me at the gym and we returned home to make the smoothie we drink each day. I worked on projects for the Omega Institute, made and received phone calls, got irritated at trivia and laughed at misunderstandings. I took a break, hit golf balls, came home, shared dinner, watched the Yankees win, and turned in. Events occurred—but nothing really *happened*.

Then I reran the day and observed what happened from a different perspective. Without even a speck of conscious awareness, my body had maintained about 100,000 heart beats and 18,000 breaths in a twenty-four hour period. I walked about three miles simply by moving from one spot to another during the course of the day. Temperatures went from 62 degrees to 84 degrees. Sun, clouds, and even a brief rain shower reflected the weather pattern of the day. Sunrise in Woodstock, NY was at 6:13 am and sunset occurred precisely at 7:14 pm.

Time moved ever so slowly—and ever so consistently. How can I say "nothing happened" when the day had been filled with miracles? Conversations took place, people interacted. At the gym we saw a friend that we hadn't seen in months. We "caught up," using all the cognitive skills and memories of our combined lives to do it. And then of course there is an array of exercise machines and machines with weights we use to strengthen our bodies without much thought as to the complexity of instructions our brain employs to properly use the gym's equipment. Until the day comes that exercising in a gym is beyond our capacity, we will probably continue to take our routines for granted. Even the word *routine* smacks with disdain at the complexity of how we function in that environment.

As I pass through an entire day, where is my appreciation for the information available to me through my five senses? Stuffed behind my to-do list, if I'm being honest. To experience the world through our senses involves both work and time. It takes consciousness to have a sensory experience as our fingers touch the clothes we wear, button our shirts, or tie our shoelaces. When we truly see the world in which we live, colors become brighter, shades more distinct. Shadows blend into buildings as they cross sidewalks and mask shapes. Our potential to concentrate on our senses only holds the promise of a deeper experience if we invest energy in manifesting that experience.

In essence, no day is a day when "nothing happens" unless we are unwilling or unable to explore using the exquisite tools at our disposal. If we decline to do the work, life dulls, eroding our curiosity and squashing our creativity. This torpor shrouds our awareness, not just around today, but the day before, and the day before that, and ever backward into a haze of assumptions and entitlements.

As I start my routine today, I resolve to bring my entire being, all my consciousness, to the day-to-day moments of life. The touch of my fingers on the keyboard, the smell of hyacinth outside our kitchen window, the vividness of colors in my study, the sweet taste of the morning mix and the growling of my stomach wanting more, or perhaps different, food. My chair squeaks as I swivel, almost in rhythm with the calling of morning birds and the sounds of children.

In the song "Halley's Comet" songwriter Stuart Markus voices regret about not making the time to experience a viewing that happens once every seventy-six years. Missing Halley's Comet is, of course, a metaphor for what happens when we exist instead of live, or float rather than dive.

The bad news is the comet has left. The good news is it will come again. And the problematic news is its return isn't scheduled until 2061. Some of us will be here to witness this celestial phenomenon, but most of us won't. Perhaps we learn more about living life fully by the moments that slip away than we do from moments we have fully embraced.

With each lost moment, every missed embrace, we become less attuned to the world around us. It's as though our skin has become thicker, insensitive to all but the most direct interactions. At those moments we need a blunt confrontation rather than a delicate touch to remember who we are. And who we are includes the ineffable part of ourselves that we label as spirit.

Connecting with that spirit is the golden opportunity of this lifetime.

Spirit won't dance for you, but it invites you to dance. It won't love for you, but it invites you to love. It won't speak for you, but it invites you to speak with your own true voice. And when we say *Yes!* we no longer believe that "nothing happened."

# Footprints

Remember the game of musical chairs you played as a child? In the game, one player at a time is eliminated as twelve players circle around eleven chairs. As long as the music plays everyone keeps circling. The moment the music stops, everyone dives for a chair. The person who can't find a chair is out of the game. Now there are only ten chairs and eleven players. One chair at a time is removed until all that's left is a single chair and two players.

Round and round they go, moving slowly as they pass the front of the chair—and then rushing past as they face the chair's back. The music suddenly stops. Both dive for the single chair. Only one person wins. We never thought of the other person as the runner-up, he had lost like everyone else.

The game is just one of many ways we are tested and judged. What influence the musical chair game has on our development stands in line with all our other interactions. Collectively, they influence our behavior, but individually they are just a relic from our growing-up years. Our capacities are continually tested in school, with friends, in sports, at home, at work, in love. At some level our responses are a manifestation of what's inside us—the unique parts that distinguish us from everyone else on the planet.

We possess both common attributes and unique features. Collectively they represent the gifts with which we are born and those we have developed along the way. To be aware of how we embody these gifts requires that we also understand that these gifts live within a unique framework that feeds from a sea of emotions, rational thinking, and spontaneous actions, to create our behavior.

Our footprint is an example of our differences. I don't mean the sort we leave behind on beaches before the tide erases our presence—but the kind that is our signature mark, our unique expression. Because no one else has lived our experiences or digested them in quite the way we have, each of us is a unique being. And the complexity of our individuality is not static, but is constantly evolving as we continue to experience life. Our interactions capture a snapshot that expresses our essence at that precise moment and become part of our historical data. In turn, that data influences but does not control the precise structure of our next footprint.

Each interaction shapes us, colors our relationships, affects us in the present moment, and influences our future. People close to us exert their influence simply by anticipating the way we will respond to any particular stimulus. Even when their assessment is not accurate, we have a tendency to interact within the framework of expectations that others hold for us. If we are known for witticisms, others may find it peculiar when we choose to be quiet. For those of us known to speak in gentle terms, a sharp retort elicits surprise. Responding with spontaneity prevents us from being hostage to our past—and enables us to approach situations unbounded and unencumbered.

Even though our behavior might seem predictable based on our prior actions, there is no assurance we will act in a particular way or respond as we have before. Until the next step is taken or decision made, our choices are broad. Once we have committed, however, the selected choice now serves as a predictor of future behavior. Our actions are not random. They are the product of prior experiences plus aspects of who we are that may not be accessible even to us. We are a product of colliding and collaborating experiences, housed in a body that possesses features no one else embodies.

Our DNA is an identifying marker that demonstrates just how unique we are among seven billion people. No duplicates and no repeats. What I find astounding about the miracle of our originality is that our DNA does not change throughout our lifetimes no matter how much change may occur to our body, our mind, or our spirit. And unlike old telephone numbers, our DNA does not get recycled. Even if you were to add those people no longer living to the seven billion current inhabitants of planet earth, there would never be any duplicates or repeats. The same holds true for fingerprints. The ones that come with us at birth do not change during our lifetimes. From infancy to death, whether we weigh seven pounds or 270 pounds, our fingerprints remain traceable as ours alone.

Our DNA may make us unique—but it does not make us special. What makes us special is how well we use the gifts we have been given over our life span. We may know the direction we want to take, but too often we avoid doing the hard work required to fulfill our potential, or to use our potential to make a difference in our own life and the lives of those we love. How things turn out continues to rest on the choices we make, the questions we ask, the spaces we allow, and the arts we practice. There is no easy path or quick fix. We are engaged in a trial and error process that continues over a very long time, and our only choice is whether or not to stay the course.

The answer of how we make that decision may be informed by philosophers like Popeye the sailor man, famous for his exclamation "I yam what I yam!" What he didn't say, but might have, is that "I yam what I yam because *I was what I was.*" The *was* relates to how we came into this world before our memory faded and our past became just a mist inhibiting our view. Usually, our beginnings fade so subtly we do not even notice their loss.

Occasionally, there are lookouts who still remember. My daughter once told me about a family with a five-year old boy and a pregnant mother. The boy kept asking his mom and dad if he could have some time alone with the baby after they were back from the hospital. Mom said "sure," but had misgivings about his unusual request and a concern for sibling rivalry. Months passed and the boy did not forget. He repeated the request until his parents, with some discomfort, consented so long as the door remained open. They listened from the hall as their son went to the crib, looked down at his newborn sister, and asked quietly "Tell me about God—I'm starting to forget."

If history is a guide, we all forget, and need to start over, again and again, reminding ourselves of the path we walk and the path we want to walk. When I think about what I bring to the starting blocks, my beginning point, I am comforted by some guideposts that remind me to act in ways that reach for the best I can be, that push me to be of service, and that allow me to walk gently, listen well, and act truthfully. My starter kit looks like this :

> Laugh more. The average adult laughs 12 times a day—the child over 400.

> See opponents as partners and partners as teachers—that way your allies outnumber your foes.

> Inquire…ask why…trust that the process is more important than the answer.

> Dance, sing loudly, and often.

> Share love. No prior experience required.

> Reach for what inspires you and draw on that inspiration to guide your actions.

> Exercise tolerance; it builds capacity for really hard times.

Say thanks…be appreciative…acknowledge mistakes…don't be trapped by your past.

Find joy at least once a day—and store it away for rainy days.

Nurture your creativity; it will pay you back ten-fold.

Now, cross out what doesn't work for you in my list—and develop your own.

Polonius, Shakespeare's chief counselor to the king, had it right. "This above all: to thine own self be true. And it shall follow as the night the day, thou canst not then be false to any man…."

# Validation

After dinner at a midtown restaurant in New York, the hostess validates my parking ticket. So does the doctor's office when I park in the lot across the street. My driver's license attests to the legitimacy of my driving another ten years.

Marriage is consummated with a document more than it is sealed with a kiss. No two birth certificates are alike. Social security numbers are a solitary form of identification that follows us throughout life. Death certificates complete the validation cycle.

Even with all the record-keeping that society requires, the essence of what makes us unique individuals remains untouched. People decide who we are by what we reveal to them. We show them parts of ourselves and they assume it is the entirety of our being.

I call the visible parts of ourselves our "presented self." In this form, we try to show our strengths and hide our vulnerabilities. Our longings, our dreams, our visions, are shared with very few. And because this part of ourselves is hidden from scrutiny—even self scrutiny—our potential is stunted and we miss the beauty of who and what we can be.

We seek safety in not standing out. We gravitate toward bland colors, muted clothes, and slow gestures. We have been trained to be cautious and to avoid the enmity of venturing beyond conformity.

I'm not sure that's how we came into this world—and perhaps it is not how we want to go out. In between, everything is possible but not much is likely. To venture out means risking a lot. But to stay in place means risking everything that could be. The real breakthrough is not in making a choice, but in knowing that we have a choice to make.

A Hebrew sage once confessed that when he died, he was not afraid that God would ask him why in life he had not been more like Moses, or Isaac, or Abraham, but that God would ask him why he had not been more like himself.

"Getting to be more like me" is coming into relationship with our "Real Self." Life's journey is measured by how well we merge our presented self and our Real Self. It is never too late to start and never too early to finish. While the opportunities to practice are endless, the rewards are uncertain.

If you want certainty, let the hostess validate your parking ticket. If you want adventure, validate it yourself. Carl Hammerschlag, a psychotherapist and healer, was given the same choice when he met with his patient, a Native American shaman, in a local hospital. The shaman asked Carl if he knew how to dance. It was a strange request, but Carl obliged. He shuffled a few steps in the hospital room. The shaman chuckled and got out of bed and began to show Carl steps he had learned as a shaman. Carl was intrigued. "Will you teach me?" he asked. The shaman said "You must be able to dance if you want to heal people. I can show you the steps but you will have to hear your own music."

# Confusion

Not long ago, I experienced three events, all of which held strong emotional charges for me. The events were interconnected only by time. The first was news I received that two friends are dealing with (or perhaps dying of) cancers that had migrated from their place of origin to other places in their bodies. The news saddened me and shocked them, as their illness had given no prior warnings. Sharing the information was an announcement that life, and how we would regard each other in the future, had changed.

My friends were the ones living the experience. I was fumbling to be of service, without being in the way. My communication was mainly through emails, phone calls, and offers to visit. My friends were all in their seventies, so the circumstances did not merit the rage one might feel when children die before their parents and the natural order of things is reversed.

We know how to celebrate birth better than we understand how to honor loss. For several months before a baby's arrival we give showers, pass on wisdom, ask about names, and watch a mom's changing anatomy. At the end of life we hold memorial services and reminisce over a friend's passing. But we are at a loss to understand the process of dying (a week, a month, a year), or how to honor time as flow rather than disjointed communication.

The second event involved a one-week memoir-writing program attended by twenty-four participants in an intimate and emotionally charged setting built around a series of writings we wrote, and read, under the watchful eye of Omega faculty member Nancy Aronie. I've taken lots of courses at Omega that were equally charged, but none of them involved an ongoing connection once the Omega program ended. Nancy's course had a life of its own, post-program. Emails were exchanged, a group system was put in place, and conversations flew back and forth.

In the campus program, Nancy had invited us to write about intimate and charged parts of our lives, often painful, unhealed, raw, and just below the surface of the civility we show to the world. We were hungry for listeners, if only to bear witness to those events that have shaped us, scarred us, or maimed us. What trust it took to tease the stories out, every tale reminding us that our own twisted path was interwoven with the paths of all the writers in the room. By Friday we shared an illusion of healing, but by the next Monday we knew our gains were smaller. We had started on the path of repairing, recovering, and restoring the core of who we are, even as we continued to live within the damage of what had been stolen from us.

The emotions released by the writing program were far removed from the emotions associated with the struggles of friends and cancer. I felt profound guilt at enjoying the pleasures of the writing course at the same time that intimates of mine were engaged in a fierce struggle for survival.

The third event was just a whisper of sounds in my ear, saying "pay attention." Attention to life, to those we love, and to joy. It involved a quiet evening at home just following the Aronie writing program. Helen and I were talking after dinner about the course, about our friends, and about us. The word that comes to mind is "appreciation"—such a quiet word, lacking splendor or fireworks. In that moment, I knew I was blessed, regardless of what tomorrow might bring.

The word "Confusion" as the title describes a sorting and blending process that I do not understand but am prepared to trust. All three events touched me in ways that were both familiar and unique. Familiar because their vibration struck common chords that yielded a sound I recognized. I know that sound from yesterday, and the day before yesterday, and from all the yesterdays that started in infancy, and hurtled me forward through all the intervening years until they came to rest in this moment. That sound is a calling, the wail I brought into this earth. Over the years I have refined and shaped and molded that chord, but it is mine and mine alone. That chord will be the last sound I hear on earth.

Each of us has a sound unique to us. We are both soloist and chorus. At any time, our chord can burst forth and be heard as separate from all the other chords of the world. It is our métier, our individual shout-out, our unique vibration that is our signature. But we are also a chorus, with all the vibrations blending and weaving into a single unity. That unity, greater than the sum of its parts, is without rancor or division. It is a note so powerful, so joyful, that its sound can reach to the edges of the universe. Perhaps there is another way to preserve our planet and save our humanity. But until we find that other path, let us live as one chorus.

# Stone Wall

I grew up with Robert Frost's poem "Mending Wall." The image Frost created describes the spring ritual of repairing the stone wall that separated his property from his neighbor's. Even as the repair work goes on, Frost comments on the winter's damage. "Something there is that doesn't love a wall, that wants it down." The neighbor, in turn, leans on his father's assurance that "Good fences make good neighbors."

Frost plays an imaginary conversation in his mind in which he asks, "Before I built a wall I'd ask to know what I was walling in or walling out, and to whom I was like to give offense." We could dally all day on that inquiry, the places in ourselves where we erect walls to hide our anger, or sadness, or grief, or loneliness. As for me, it is part of my nature to construct walls, perhaps more like labyrinths, with complex pathways to the center of my heart. That center is open and vulnerable. When I sense danger, I move into lockdown mode, with little passing in or out, save for the peepholes from which I monitor the dangers I perceive, and ask to know who seeks access to my heart.

The heart is the fifth largest organ in the body. We consider feelings and emotions to stem from or be stored in the heart, our receptacle for love, pain, fear, spirit and desire. Anthropologist and spiritual teacher Angeles Arrien described the health of the four chambers of the heart by their ability to be

Clear hearted, not confused

Full hearted, not half-hearted

Open hearted, not closed

Strong hearted, not weak

Imagine if we began each morning by checking in with our heart to gauge how clear, full, open and strong we were at that moment. Such a commitment would guide our actions, our words, our behavior, and our intentions. Imagine further, if you will, what might happen if we set an intention to strengthen those chambers that were fragile or in disrepair.

We could, as an exercise, work on a chamber each morning, testing, repairing, loving what is, and in each moment of the day, encourage the fullness of what that quality might become, to blossom. We need to know how we undermine or sabotage our heart, and then fill our chambers with forgiveness. When we are too angry or stubborn or too afraid, we become disconnected from our heart. With that attitude, I'm erecting walls within myself against the feelings churning inside. I have become incapable of intimacy and unable to resolve what needs closure or to heal what is injured.

If our shutdown affected only ourselves, we might

mourn the loss of an opportunity. But, truth be told, we are an interdependent species. Our affect ripples out over all we meet, corroding relationships and damaging other hearts. When our heart is clear, full, open and strong, that too ripples out and washes over those we meet. We are not only healing ourselves, we are healing humanity, person by person.

It is common to believe that the health of our heart depends on the strength or wisdom of others. Many of us engage in an eternal search for teachers, only to find ourselves disappointed in the teachers we find. Most of us recognize our limitations more easily than we acknowledge our strengths. Even worse, we exaggerate our limitations and minimize our strengths. Where then do we look for support that transforms risk and provides us with the mantle of protection so we can open our hearts in safety?

Young children have superheroes that come to the rescue, like the Tooth Fairy and Sandman. As we mature, we adopt superheroes from the Marvel comics, like Spiderman, Batman, and Wonder Woman. As adults, many of us seek wisdom from figures such as psychics, channels, and mediums.

We ask too much and they tell us too little. The wisdom shared from beyond may inform our hearts, but it cannot repair what is broken inside of us. Repair work is the work of a lifetime. It takes an inner journey traveled over a lifetime to make external changes in the world. Those changes require our walls to be dismantled, our doorways to be opened, and our love to emanate from the core of our being.

The gods are not out there, they are within us, and it is time to wake them up. The Buddhist expression *Namaste* means *I honor the god within you.* When we can hold the other in that image, the wisdom imparted from the other side will be the wisdom of the heart, and we will be our own super-heroes.

# Yes and No

Early in life we create patterns of behavior that turn into habits. From experience we know that habits are hard to break. Infants learn to say no before they learn to say yes, a response that becomes more ingrained as we grow older. When faced with choices, adults have a tendency to lean into saying no before taking a breath and considering what saying yes might be like. I recognize there are various meanings and shadings that can be attributed to the word no and times when using that word reflects a decision reached after thoughtful examination. I also know there are other times when our rapid answer has precluded any serious consideration.

When saying no is a reflexive response, we are protecting the status quo of our life. I find it curious that for so many people their first instinct is to protect that status quo, even when the life they have is not the life they envision. We may be influenced to say no because what we hear is not really what is being offered, particularly when the offer sets off warning bells grounded in historical fears If you look at recent decisions you've made, consider what part of your no was rooted in fear and what part was a thoughtful response. Distinguishing between those two polar opposites— a premature rejection  and a serious exploration—requires us to be both wise and insightful. With wisdom we learn from earlier mistakes. With insight we anticipate them.

In improvisation, you never say no to a statement made to you during a scene. Responding with a no is the death knell that stifles dialogue and dampens energy. Even when you leave the door ajar by modifying the response so that you actually say *no, but...* it's a show stopper of the wrong kind. Your job in improvisation is to make the other person appear to be brilliant, and move the dialogue along through invitation rather than denial. Saying *yes* or even *yes and...* flings the door wide open so that routines can flourish in many directions.

Recently I spent a quiet hour thinking back on some seminal decisions I made as a young adult, and the shadow cast by my family of origin over my own inclinations and the struggle I endured to follow my own instincts. One decision lay before me as my senior class in college neared graduation—what to do after I had my diploma. I could work, attend graduate school, travel the world, take a fling at theatre, or try writing. Today that seems a rich brew from which to have chosen. Back then I felt velcroed to a career path and saw my options narrowed to one—attendance at my choice of a graduate school. I narrowed my next step to either enrolling in law school at Columbia or Yale. I made lists of the relative benefits and detriments of a degree from each university. I weighed each item on the list. In short, I drew up a battle plan for the wrong war. My real battle was with geography. Would I commute to school or leave home for school? Until I understood the core issue, I favored Columbia. Once I understood the stakes, Yale became my school of choice.

Having started on a career path in the law, my choices came rapidly. Did I want to work in a large firm or a small one; would I practice as a generalist or a specialist; would my work be done in an urban setting or a rural one? Those opportunities, and the decisions I made regarding them, influenced my character, values, and personality, and stretched far beyond issues governing career. When I look back, I can see the essence of who I am today in the form of who I was when I struggled with those decisions. Years have allowed the dross to wash away and the underlying metal to be more visible.

Over that time there have been thousands of choices requiring yes or no decisions to be made. Those choices have been messy, uneven, and often mistake-filled. But they have also allowed me to see parts of myself that make up my essential core, often surprising me and leaving me in awe of who I can be when I get out of my own way.

Perhaps we could undertake exercises that would help us see what part of our history has an undue influence on our choices. We might, at the start of such an inquiry, list the hang ups that afflict us so much that they smother our own voice in favor of voices from our past. Once acknowledged, move on. Find your cushion and sit. By that I mean, locate a quiet space, schedule no other activity, turn off your email, and put your cell phone away.

As you wait for a decision to embrace you, consider the story of a rabbi in a small town in Eastern Europe. The town bully accosts the rabbi in the town square. "You're so smart," smirks the bully. "Tell me if the bird in my hand is alive or dead." The rabbi immediately realizes that if he says alive, the bully will squeeze the bird trapped in his palm and let it fall lifelessly to the ground. And if the rabbi says that the bird is dead, the bully will open his palm and let the bird fly away. Trapped by the way his choices had been circumscribed, the rabbi responds simply. "The answer is up to you."

And so it is.

# More Thoughts on Yes and No

Life is quite familiar to us when *no* is our operative word for trolling through life. When *yes* is our operative word, life becomes an adventure that brings together a host of feelings that emerge whenever a component of change is included. If you are confused, I have listed just a few of the likely outcomes that may relate to your decision. The list is not exhaustive; please add to my list of polar opposites by creating your own.

When no is a fortress, yes is undefended.

When no is impenetrable, yes is vulnerable.

When no is opaque, yes is transparent.

When no is a caution, yes is a risk.

When no is shutting down, yes is opening up.

When no is a separation, yes is a connection.

# Section 4

# Blessing

May we remember to be kinder.

May we remember to be gentler.

May we teach our children to listen with their hearts,

And by so teaching, may we listen for our own heart's song.

May we smile more, breathe more deeply, walk slower, and help sooner.

On matters of principle, may we stand in the water like a rock,

And in matters of love, may we follow the stream like a petal.

May we not waste a minute, but never hurry.

May we not be distracted, but always open.

May our lives be uncluttered, but filled with memories.

# Decoys

I woke up this morning thinking about decoys. Insofar as they involve wildlife, they hold little interest for me. But when I consulted the Miriam-Webster dictionary and read the definition, "someone or something used to lure or lead another into a trap," I realized that decoys were mirroring something urgent in my life—perhaps in all our lives.

Decoys imitate life, but they are not life itself. They are durable, clever, disguised, repetitive, inviting, and treacherous. Decoys constantly throw themselves in our path. We think *how attractive—how interesting*. We don't look at their underbellies to examine how they are made. Have we failed in our ability to separate fact from illusion or have we just ignored the signals that shout *Caution!* What our heart truly desires is an acceptance of blunders we make in persuing false values and patience as we grope for truths.

In Greek history, the Trojan horse symbolized the difference between appearance and reality, and its story is responsible for the proverb that we should *"beware of Greeks bearing gifts."* In his travels, Odysseus is warned to resist the call of the Sirens if he is to avoid certain destruction. As Odysseus's ship sails towards the Sirens and their enticing sounds, the ship is in danger of foundering on the rocks. Odysseus orders his men to bind him to the mast, and no matter how he begs or implores them to remove the bindings, he is not to be released until the ship sails safely past the music of the Sirens. All the crew members are instructed to fill their ears with beeswax to block out the sounds of the Siren song and steer a steady course to safety.

Today's decoys may be more subtle, but are no less destructive. Haven't we all heard sounds that tempt us to leave our path? We can be drawn in by promises that our dreams will be realized and our ambitions met. One more try, one more effort, and surely we will succeed. Sometimes we do…and sometimes we don't. But either way, the music lures us onward toward the rocks.

Decoys exist in the work we do and the relationships we forge. They invite us to tangle with life by investing our time and committing our energy to certain goals. If we are wise, we will examine the return we expect to receive on the investment we make. Sometimes it's a paycheck or a position of power. Sometimes it's a partnership built on convenience instead of conviction. And sometimes it's an energetic bond so powerful that nothing can rend it apart. We need to explore whether our return is the real thing, an element of our being, or a decoy that is merely trappings.

I have found that decoys stunt our growth. If we want to grow, we must invite passion into our lives, search relentlessly for the essence of who we are, identify what make us unique, and offer it to the world with a humility born of trial and error.

We need to ask ourselves *if I give this up, will I still be me? Can I compromise my integrity and still know myself? Can I turn a blind eye and not diminish who I am?* As we find the pieces of ourselves that simply cannot be surrendered, we have found a way to distinguish our personal decoys from the essential form they imitate.

By asking these questions and paying attention to the responses, we begin to recognize the decoys in our lives and what urges us forward in their pursuit. Each time I identify a decoy that I am ready to surrender, I store it in the trophy room of my mind. Each decoy exposed and discarded brings me closer to Self, closer to essence, closer to the divine. As the room fills with the decoys I have shed, they mark my personal journey and I treasure them as evidence of a life well lived.

# Dissonance

When Daniel got a new set of drums for the holidays, we all shared in the consequences. Ear-splitting background noise, followed by short pauses, followed by phone calls to Daniel's parents. Now we had to negotiate. How late could he play, how often could he play, how loud could he play? Our compromise was four hours a day, no later than nine pm, no limit on noise, and a renegotiation should he ever have a gig for which he needed to practice.

I'm a crummy negotiator. I wanted capital punishment for violation of our agreement, perhaps a scalding of fingers so they would need to be wrapped up for weeks at a time. All of life is a series of lessons. I learned I like my quiet, that I distract easily, and that I don't appreciate invasions of my space.

Daniel offered me an opportunity to think about why we push away anything we feel is dissonant and long for it to vanish. There is a connection between the amount of dissonance we live with and the state of our well-being. In fact, Daniel presents only one very simple form of dissonance. Other forms affect our view of the world and leave us in an uncomfortable state when our beliefs and values are challenged by opposing positions. No one likes to be in such a state. When confronted, we try different approaches to bring disparate views into consonance. Just as cacophony is the alter ego of euphony, so consonance is the opposite of dissonance.

How much dissonance we can tolerate may depend on our makeup. Certain kinds of dissonance do not infect the core of who we are and can be tolerated more easily than the kinds of dissonance that feel like a mortal shot burrowing into the center of our being. But when the discomfort does not dissolve, we suffer it with a continual itch until we discover where to scratch.

Imagine if we could piece together a life without conflict or inner turmoil. You may think such an existence is idyllic, but you would be wrong. What may appear desirable as an idea tanks in practice. Without conflict, growth is stunted, there is no appreciation of differences, and no reaching of a synthesis drawn from competing strands in a rug pattern.

Conflicts occur daily. Some evaporate with time, while others are more persistent and require attention. Here are some places where dissonance frequently shows up:

> *In relationships.* Are we looking for sex or love? Passion or faithfulness? Desire or satisfaction?

> *In work.* Do we want a paycheck or meaning? Do we try to be a difference maker or settle for being a cog in someone else's machine?

> *When it feels as if life is either dragging us backward or thrusting us forward.* How do we appreciate the

present moment? How do we avoid living in the time zone of "what was" or "what will be" and enter into the enormity of "what simply is?"

*When we are afraid to express our true nature.* How do we find a way to act as we believe and not how others believe we should act? How can we bring our true nature out of hiding to relieve anxiety and stay trustworthy?

Sometimes we are the source of the dissonance. We quit one job to take another, move from one city to another, end or start a new relationship. Sometimes we are faced with changes we did not create. Our job is terminated and we need to find another; we suffer a loss and our balance is off. In either case, dissonance is not the event, but the consequence of the event. We have choices and choices change the status quo. We hope the change will diminish the dissonance, but we can never be certain until we experience how the changed environment feels.

If dissonance seems an unfamiliar term, try substituting the word *stress*. My hesitancy in using that word stems from the fact that there are so many forms and types of stress, from acute to general, and from current to flashbacks, we could get lost just in trying to agree on a definition. It is important to realize that stress is not just a way of life. It is one of life's signals. We can ameliorate some stress by altering the nature of the work we choose to do or the relationships we perpetuate within our family units. But stress never dissolves completely or disappears entirely.

In most of my writings, this is the place where I try and share an "aha" moment of insight, suggest a rebalancing exercise when life threatens to go off the rails, or offer a crutch to survive the dark moments. But the truth is that I am in the same quandary as you when it comes to finding anchors to keep us from drifting off in directions that aren't productive or chasing after solutions that do not address the angst of daily life.

What I do know is that stress is universal. It may be reflected in a thousand forms, but it is a common thread we share. If we watch how others respond to their stresses, we may learn a bit about handling our own.

We all have values we try to incorporate into our lives, but our ability to live those values is often thwarted by compromises we make. The degree of stress with which we live is related to how well our actions reflect our values. When we devote significant energy to actions that don't advance how we want to model our lives, one of the prices we pay is an increased stress level.

Sometimes we think we understand what is causing us distress and we set out to make important shifts. If we are too abrupt in interrupting old patterns, we may create new stresses as powerful as the ones we seek to replace. If we can moderate the changes we are trying to initiate by leaning on our friends, moving at a measured pace, or sitting in meditation on our cushion, we may be able to smooth out the bumps caused by major changes in lifestyle.

Life is too serious to be lived without humor. I have learned how essential it is to find time to laugh, especially at yourself, and see how the burdens we carry can be lightened. Once a day is a good beginning.

Life lightens immeasurably when we include a daily dose of beauty. That beauty can take the form of a landscape, a painting, a favorite poem, or a writing that moves us. Beauty is an eternal counterbalance to daily suffering, but it needs conscious action by us to be an antidote to the tensions of daily living. For me, beauty is the poetry of John O'Donahue, the lyrics of Harry Chapin, the music of Stephen Sondheim, the writings of Wallace Stegner, and the friends I have made over a lifetime.

Love is the connection point that dissolves the defenses that separate us from each other. The energy of love is drawn to the places and spaces where it is invited; it stays so long as it is honored and remembered. When we engage love, we are transmuting what is dissonant in our lives into what is consonant.

I look back at the discoveries I have made about stress over many years and the steps I have taken to counterbalance its effect. Grading my own performance is a bad idea. A better idea would be to eliminate grades altogether in favor of compassion. How about trusting how I feel, not how I think? That's my mantra for the future. I'll let you know how I'm doing if you tell me how it's going for you.

# Rituals

Words in common hang around together. They relate to each other but stretch in slightly different directions. Their nuances make our language sufficiently rich that we never run out of ways to provide new descriptions for old thoughts and ideas. When I began writing this reflection, I wanted to focus on what we mean when we talk about *habit*. Then other words, such as tradition, custom, ceremony, and ritual, made better fits in some places, and worse in others, as a substitute for the word habit. As I parsed my way through different options, I felt at risk of strangling my writing and beating it senseless in my struggle for clarity. I decided, as a survival technique, to use words that met my own sense of nuance, even adding the word *treasure* as a placeholder for some of the ideas described below.

I come from a family that honored certain traditions, mainly centered around food and holidays, such as Rosh Hashanah and Passover. Growing up, I had little regard for the events themselves because it always seemed we were honoring the food instead of the food honoring the event. As a friend once commented, we seemed to be culinary Jews—families that gathered for food that we tied to a holiday, with scant attention paid to the holiday itself.

I see now I had been shortsighted, and perhaps a little self-righteous. It was the act of breaking matzah (or bread) that was the ritual that honored our Jewish heritage. I believe this is true for many Jewish households around the world. Jews have been celebrating these holidays in every corner of the planet for thousands of years, and our small dinners contributed to sustaining a shared belief that celebrating in this way helped keep our tradition alive. It didn't matter that we did it badly or gave short shrift to the religious meaning behind the food we served. It mattered that we wanted in.

I call those kinds of traditions treasures of the heart. They feel good, connect us to our heritage, tie us to history, and remind us that habits can share a common pulse. Treasures of the heart can be outgoing and open, or can be small and intimate. Sometimes they are supported by one generation for many years until future generations assume responsibility. Sons hold Seders that fathers attend; daughters light candles on Friday night, offering prayers their mothers had taught them; and friends make room for friends at holiday time.

Growing up I never appreciated that the way my mother set the table and prepared the food served as her own form of prayer. At Rosh Hashanah, our good china was placed around the table, together with silverware that had been polished to a sheen and stemware that was only used three times a year. No one interfered in the kitchen; the kitchen was my mother's domain. Only later did I appreciate the effort she expended to shop, cook, and clean, and at the end of a festive night put back the china, reshelve the silverware, and return the stemware to the kitchen cabinets where they were stored until the next ritual celebration.

Families also create unique treasures of the heart that bind them together by continual repetition. For many years I was an overworked lawyer fighting to find time for my wife and children. When my oldest daughter was five, we initiated a ritual that an entire day would belong just to Dana and me. We would start as early as she liked, go anywhere she wanted, and stay out as late as she requested. In the early years it was McDonald's, miniature golf, a movie, and ice cream. As the years passed, we ventured further from home, took in theatre, and dined rather than ate. When my younger daughter Amy reached the age of five, there was a special day added just for her. The girls thought they owned the universe on those days. In reality, the universe of a father and his daughter was a gift to me. No matter how busy I was, or how pressed with work, our days together were sacred.

The more that treasures are used the deeper the experience. They touch the heart, enrich our lives, and often constitute a shared experience. One treasure of the heart that comes to mind is the creation of a "glory box." Start with a box the size of a shoe or cigar box. You can use the box "as is" or personalize it by painting some or all of its exterior, and covering it with tissue paper or collage. When completed, store the box out of the way, but in an accessible place. Into that box pour items from your past and present that have special meaning. Perhaps a poem by a writer you appreciate, such as an Irish blessing by John O'Donahue or a summer reflection by Mary Oliver. Add to your glory box a scrapbook of family photos and cards from grandchildren. All the better if there are expressions of how much you mean to others. The contents are reminders that you matter.

A glory box is the right receptacle to hold memories of acts of kindness from others that you have received, as well as kindnesses you have shown. For twenty years Helen and I lived in a co-housing community, a form of residential living where owners commit to be "good neighbors." Other residents of this community helped make us feel like we were living with extended family. There are so many good memories from that era that our challenge is not what to put into the glory box, but what can be left out.

When Helen and I decided to move West, we felt a strong wrench as we finalized our plans for leaving. The community feared that our absence would create a void with the loss of two experienced members who had been successful in resolving conflicts, listening to grievances, and living by consensus. In a sense, our contribution over time had been to mentor the community about its values rather than its limitations, focus on its strengths rather than its weaknesses, and appreciate the benefits of community rather than its costs. We know that others will step forward in our co-housing project and do as well or better than we have done—the community just doesn't know that yet.

There is another kind of treasure, with a different dimension, where treasures connect with a force beyond ourselves, rather than connect to ourselves or to others. We may think of that force as God, or spirit, or nature, or soul. What we call it is less important than knowing there is a part of us that wants to connect to the sacred, to a part of the universe that is greater than ourselves but which includes every one of us.

Finding treasures of the soul is an individual journey. Friends of mine have set aside a room, separate from the rest of the house, to practice meditation. The only furniture in that room is a set of meditation cushions and an altar in one corner of the room. They consider that meditation space as sacred, separate from the rest of the house. Others practice mindfulness, whether by sitting on their pillows or going on retreats. Helen and I have begun to take a moment before eating any meal we share, holding hands and appreciating each other, life, food, and the planet. Simple, but a bow in the direction of our intentions.

I have been part of a group that has met quarterly for almost twenty years. We meet at different homes. The host selects the opening music, after which we sit in meditation for forty-five minutes, share what is happening in our world, and then feast on a potluck meal. With our joint history, we know each other's stories. But we are there to listen. We hear about illnesses, births, struggles, occasional triumphs, difficult losses. We are there to be with each other, whether with words or in silence. It is about being part of the same experience.

I describe the experience as though Helen and I are still full participants. We are welcome to join the group at any of their meetings—but in truth that is unlikely from 3,000 miles away. I value the experience, but hurt that I have lost such an intimate connection.

When I was an adult with a growing family, I found connecting with the sacred daunting. I led a busy life, was easily distracted, and concentrated on tangible goals that related to family, work, or self. The sacred had to tuck itself into some corner of my daily menu, neither prominently displayed nor fully discarded. What I learned is that searching for the sacred is a forgiving activity. It forgives me for the years when business trumped the sacred. Now, with age and perspective, the sacred doesn't just trump business; it is how I do business.

My life lessons are mine. To the extent those treasures can serve you in any way, I offer them to you with an open heart. To the extent your treasures might entwine with mine, I remain open to learning from them. I understood after many years the difference between living *in* the present moment and living *for* the present moment. I learned that sacred space doesn't have to be in my home, but it must occupy a corner of my heart. In the years when I built a fortress of resistance, all the sacred spaces I envisioned in my home gathered

dust until my heart could open again to grace and
forgiveness. In those moments when my heart flies
open, my connection to the sacred feels complete.

# Habits

I recently Googled the word *habit* (which in itself could be habit-forming) to learn a bit about methods used by so-called authorities to create and break habits. I read a variety of reports that offered suggestions on how to form or break habits, and what brain activities are stimulated when we go on automatic pilot and enter into an habitual state. When I finished, I felt that the methods listed seemed less like science and more like folklore.

The effects of a habit can be neutral, devastating or desirable. For example, I consider waking up at the same time each day a neutral activity. Waking up and reaching for a first cigarette of the day is courting the risk of cancer. Waking up and going to the gym or practicing morning meditation, from my perspective, are desirable activities.

Typical habits may involve driving to and from work, a daily task generally carried out at the same time each week. We drive familiar roads, and hardly recall how we got to our destination. Once our driving routine kicks in, we are able to multitask by bringing our attention to the radio, carrying on a conversation, or playing over in our minds some issue that has caught our attention. Making the morning call to aging parents can also become a habit—like a "to do" check list of activities to be accomplished, with little appreciation for the reasons behind the call or the activity.

Initially, the part of our brain that is known as the prefrontal cortex is the place where decisions are made. As the same activity becomes automatic, the decision-making part of the brain goes into a sort of sleep mode, and another part of the brain, the basal ganglia, plays a key role in pattern recognition. Repeat the same activity enough times and you are creating a habit that the brain hardly has to acknowledge in order to accomplish the task.

I consider operating on automatic pilot risky business, particularly when it relates to interpersonal relations. We may tell our partner every morning that we love her. Miss a day and someone's feelings are hurt. Say it enough days and you risk losing the essence of the message. You can address this issue by changing a detail, perhaps by altering the lilt in your voice, the time when you deliver the message, the note you leave when you go to work early, or the email you write when you take a coffee break.

As important as it is to express feelings, it's critical to show them. We need to be alert to our feelings, as well as the sounds and sights and smells and images around us. We need to appreciate the importance of the human touch and how it expresses warmth and intimacy. If you own a dog, you will see in your pet a living example of how fresh a greeting can be when you come home from work (or even return from just a short trip to the grocery). Dogs don't stop at a perfunctory bark because for them the world has been born anew. Master is home and that simply is the best feeling in the world. Not just for the dog, but for you as well.

Habits are devoid of warmth. By their very nature, habits have a semi-autonomous nature that separates the action being taken from the underlying sensations that accompany it. When we are in habit-mode, it's easy to miss the moment of beauty because we are in a hurry, or because we are preoccupied, or because we have transformed our caring into a routine instead of a vibrant and unique expression of our feelings.

What if the moment passes without engaging us in the experience? Have we traded the opportunity to connect for the convenience of habitual action? Has the opportunity for a sacred moment slipped away? While other moments will certainly appear in their stead, sacred moments are not interchangeable. They are more like snowflakes; each shares a common beauty, yet the configuration of every snowflake is unique.

Parents whose children attended the Newtown school will recall forever last words shared with a child. Children who were not victims will have been held tighter that night, loved harder, and truly valued as sacred beings. Does it take adversity to remind us that attention is the doorway to presence? When we are on automatic pilot, we risk losing sacred opportunities by converting them into actions we barely recognize. As we pull back to center, we serve ourselves and those we love by living our sacred moments to their fullest expression.

I am concerned that we frequently act out of habit without understanding what the cost of habitual action might be. Habits don't have to be activities performed by rote. They can be activities based on expectations grounded in roles, such as exists between employer and employee, parent and child, or teacher and student. The ruts grooved by playing a role again and again can imprison participants as though they were actors confined to lines in a script. When we expect behavior to adhere to traditional roles, we undervalue our independent spirit, spontaneity, and innocence.

There is a Zen parable in which traditional roles are used as a teaching opportunity. In the story, a monk is interrupted in prayer by a tall, scowling Samurai who exclaims, "Monk—I have no time for your slow-winded ways. Teach me about heaven and hell—and do it now." The monk looks up at the red face of the Samurai and responds, "Teach you? You are arrogant, rude, you smell, and lack manners." The monk laughs in the face of the Samurai. "Teach you? I'd sooner teach a monkey." This response so enraged the Samurai that he pulled his great sword from its scabbard, intending to plunge it into the monk to eviscerate him. Then, at the last possible moment the monk looked into the eyes of the Samurai, and said quietly "That which you are now experiencing is hell."

The Samurai's sword hung in mid-air. Realizing that

the monk was indeed teaching him what he had asked for, even at the risk of his own life, he bursts into tears, overwhelmed by the generosity of the monk. Gently, he lay the sword at the feet of the monk in deep appreciation. "And that," said the monk, "is heaven."

When we perform our roles in habitual ways, the opportunities to alter the outcome are limited, but they do appear. Ignore the chance to change our usual conduct and the monk is sacrificed and the Samurai has learned nothing. If we can conduct ourselves so as to look for moments of change, and act on them, we change the Samurai in us forever.

# Spare Change

*Hey bud, you got some spare change to share? Don't want no moralizing, no woulda, coulda, shoulda. Just some change rattling round your pocket I'm asking you to share. It used to be a dime got me some coffee and a buck bought me a snort. Now your spare change doesn't buy a lot. Truth is, I get tired of asking, but sure could use that buck. You get tired of giving?*

Spare change—the coins we put on our table after we empty our pockets. Change from the cleaners, the coffee shop, the haircut, and, oh yeah, the bar at 6 o'clock. Usually I don't give it much thought. Spare change is about weight, not value. I look at each piece of change I have littered onto the nightstand and wonder about weight. Pound and a half, easy, even after a fistful went to the homeless guy on the corner near my house. But tonight I can't shake the guy who asked me for spare change. I could throw away some change nightly, and it wouldn't matter to me. But to him, at that moment, it's everything.

There's my story, there's his story, and there's a story behind the spare change. Each coin has a history. Take the penny. When no one's looking, people discard them as having no value anymore. When referring to a penny, we're not talking money. A penny is just a figure of speech, a form of social interaction. Because it has so little value as currency, we are able to load the penny up with all sorts of social messages. When we tell someone "a penny for your thoughts" we are talking about a currency of the heart, not a value of the mind.

In England, people chant about the holiday spirit:

> Christmas is coming, the goose is getting fat.
> Please put a penny in the old man's hat.
> If you haven't got a penny then a ha'penny will do.
> And if you haven't got a ha'-penny, then
> God bless you.

Salvation in the form of kind acts. Maybe we should commit daily to as many kind acts as we have pennies in our pocket.

So why not just take the penny out of circulation? Because it lives deep within our history, and is a reminder of what used to have value. It's like a piece of clay we can twist to form whatever shape we want, and whatever expression we need. Maybe that's the reason for asking the checkout clerk to let full payment slide when you're two cents short and don't want pennies as change for a nickel. Enlightened stores now have a cup with pennies and customers are invited to take, or leave, their extra pennies. That way no one looks cheap or is pushing an edge. The store won't miss it, I won't miss it, and the clerk won't miss it.

I see four nickels on the nightstand. For people who

can't tell a kumquat from an Idaho potato, the advice not to take a plugged nickel may fall on deaf ears. But a warning is a warning. Don Corleone put a horse's head in a rival's bed when an upstart threatened to encroach on the Don's territory. A plugged nickel may have the same effect. A marksman puts a hole in the center of a nickel, ruining the coin but sending an eloquent message that you could be next. That way you don't have to get rid of the rest of the horse. And it's easier to keep a pocket full of plugged nickels than a stable of horses. Ultimately, being told that *anything you do isn't worth a plugged nickel* would be message enough for me to consider changing careers and finding a new location away from horses.

Dimes are the thinnest coin made by the U.S. mint. Light in the pocket and light on the table. The dimes I'm looking at all have FDR's profile. Back in 1920, FDR contracted polio. He raised money for a charity that he named the National Foundation for Infantile Paralysis. I remember the back story.

Edward Israel Iskowitz helped raise money for this charity. In 1938, he asked the country on his radio show to join a program called the March of Dimes. This program asked listeners to send their dimes to support FDR's original foundation under its new name—the March of Dimes. In that year alone, 2,680,000 dimes made their way to the White House and Franklin's charity. No wonder FDR's image is on that coin. The feel-good ending to a crippling disease was the invention of a vaccine by Jonas Salk that has virtually wiped out polio in the United States and most European countries. People still remember Edward Israel Iskowitz today, but they remember him as Eddie Cantor. If you don't know who Eddie Cantor is—ask Siri.

But the dime ain't worth what it used to be. The guy on the corner begging for spare change needs a lot more dimes these days just to get a cup of coffee. He's really an alchemist. In my pocket coins are spare change. In his they are a lifeline for food and drink.

When we get to the quarter we're beginning to talk real money. The quarter was the coin of choice for parking meters and public phones before credit cards became an alternative method of payment and required more than a high school degree to operate. It's also the coin most coveted at commercial laundries for activating the washer or dryer.

When we talk about quarters, I remember Uncle Jack, one of my Dad's five brothers-in-law. Whenever the families got together, at least 20 relatives showed up for dinner and schmoozing, Uncle Jack included. The women loved it—the gossip, the worrying, the support and understanding, the concerns about having a job, making dollars stretch, bewilderment over how to raise children, and what to do about acting-out teenagers. My aunts were cooks, eager to teach the next generation how to prepare food, and the next generation rebelled against learning. We kids tolerated these gatherings, and the husbands hated them. The men usually left as a single body, with Uncle Julie leading the way, for bowling and pizza.

Not Uncle Jack. He slept through most of the gatherings, sleep made easier because he was conveniently deaf. But before he zoned out in the recliner rocker, he'd pull me aside and proceed to twist my ear until quarters fell out of my head and into his hand. Somehow I never got to keep those quarters, even though they'd been dug out of *my* head and *my* ear.

At night, when my family was in bed, I'd sneak into the bathroom and shake my head: it was just possible that quarters were still stuffed inside. But all my pulling, plucking, pleading, and twisting failed to loosen any quarters and have them tumble into the sink. I think I got close a few times, but never hit the jackpot the way Jack could. By the time I reached an age when I understood it was sleight of hand, it no longer mattered. I graduated to join Uncle Julie's crew and go for bowling and pizza with the men. There was a rhythm and ritual to the gatherings, which continued until too many of my aunts and uncles got too sick from being too old. They're all dead now, but Uncle Jack's trickster personality is an indelible composite of our family gatherings. It's a pity I never got to ask him where he learned his magic, and if it made him truly happy.

Fifty-cent pieces are coins of conscience. They're too big to get lost in the corners of your purse or hide in the bowels of your pocket. Drop a hand in and you feel them right away. When the homeless man stops you on the street and asks for spare change, and your fingers tighten on the half-dollar, do you extract it from your pocket or roam around searching for coins of lesser value?

The half-dollar is just the right size for a modern day equivalent to the Roman coin that was either placed over the mouth or eyes of the deceased The coin was used to pay Charon, the ferryman who was believed to transport souls across the river Styx to the other side after the spirit had moved on. It was folklore that if you had no coin to pay Charon, you wandered around for 100 years until you could find your way to the other side. No one should die without money to pay Charon.

I slip on my shoes, gather up all the spare change from the nightstand and head for the street. I'm looking for the guy who had asked me for some earlier, but he's gone for the night. I go back home, knowing that the spare change in my pocket isn't mine to keep—I'm only the bag man holding it for him.

# Time and Space

We are mesmerized by speed. Breaking the four-minute mile was considered physically impossible, at least until 1954 when Roger Bannister ran that distance in just a fraction faster than four minutes. Once he demonstrated that the barrier was psychological and not physical, thirty-seven other runners went through that portal in the same year. Thousands more have accomplished a sub-four-minute mile since Bannister's breakthrough run. Their speed is measureable at 15 miles per hour. Olympic sprinter Usain Bolt's world record speed translates into about 27 mph, fast for a human. The cheetah can travel short distances at speeds up to 60 mph, and no animal moves faster.

In other realms, the speed of light provides interesting observations. Let's assume that a star is a million light years away from earth. That means the light from that star traveled for a million years until we could see it. Anything about that light is old news—yesterday's story. If we want to know what is happening on that star today, we'll need to wait another million years to find out. Our sun is closer to home. What occurs on the sun only takes eight minutes to reach us. But the break between events and observance is always eight minutes behind real-time occurrences.

At a summer camp many years ago, my daughter Dana had to write her mom and dad on her first night away. After the obligatory comments on how wonderful camp was, she informed us about the sleeping arrangements. It seemed she was assigned the top bunk of a two-tiered frame and was badly frightened that she would hurt herself getting in or out of bed. That first letter to us made us wonder if we had picked the wrong camp. We immediately called the owner, who promised to switch her bunk right away. Next morning we got a call from the owner. When he had given Dana the choice of switching beds, she had no recollection of writing to us, of being scared, or of wanting to make a change. We were reacting to something that had taken place earlier in time, and treated it as having occurred with the arrival of the letter—not its mailing.

Had texting been invented at that time, we would have dealt with the issue in real time, but perhaps we would have lost something by not letting time disarm a loaded situation or allow the sort of resolution that comes when we give space to a problem.

We live in an era where immediate responses are the norm. We have ushered into life the technology of emails, text messages, Instagrams, Tweets, and YouTube. The expectations created by these forms of communication are not likely to be reversed. In fact, I fully expect several more breakthroughs achieved in my lifetime will affect not only what we do, but who we are. In that world, you get what you pay for. Often, quick responses are short on facts, long on emotions, confused about message, and devoid of thoughtful rumination. On the other hand, responses do appear more rapidly. In certain circumstances a quick expression of feelings can keep misunderstandings from festering and facilitate clarity. In other circumstances, the opposite can happen.

As a lawyer I used to joke with colleagues in negotiating sessions that the person who stopped to draw a breath first became the designated listener. We have lost the art of good listening. It requires skill, attention, and commitment. Too often, when we are in dialogue with someone, we listen for a pause in their rhetoric so we can whisk into the empty space and voice our opinion, instead of taking the time to hear them out, consider their position, and respond thoughtfully.

How, then, do we incorporate into our lives the compassion that emerges from true listening? How do we replace agendas with conversations, attitudes with curiosity, and restrictions with inclusion? The Buddhists have been practicing how to be fully present for 2,500 years, ever since Siddhartha vowed to sit under the Bodhi tree until he achieved enlightenment, meditating on his in-breath and his out-breath, a form of meditation that invites us to follow both the in-breath and the out-breath, to be aware of the breath that is breathing us, not change or alter it…simply be aware of it.

Think about it. When we take an in-breath we are unable to speak. Our physiological makeup demands a choice: speak or breathe, but not both in the same instant. Breathing in creates the space for real dialogue by slowing the rhythm and allowing us to notice what is occurring around us and within us. We can concentrate on pairing our feelings and our words, because the in-breath offers us time to be aware of both.

Slowing down my own rhythm lets me be more myself. It invites me to understand how my thoughts reflect who I am. Consider the following:

> The thought manifests as the word;
> The word manifests as the deed;
> The deed develops into habit;
> And habit hardens into character.
> So watch the thought and its ways with care
> And let it spring from love
> Born out of concern for all beings.
> (Author unknown)

We often praise speeches by acknowledging how wonderful they are. Let us also praise audiences that listen intently.

# Section 5

# Blessing

There is a state of mind that is gravitationally drawn toward an expression we all recognize: *when I see it—I'll believe it.* It is a time honored viewpoint that respects what is concrete. The images conjured up are steadfast and true, incontrovertible and factual. It is a cousin of the sales pitch that tells us *what you see is what you get.*

Alter the mantra ever so slightly and the expression, rephrased, says *when I believe it, I'll see it.* Suddenly our state of mind expands into a state of imagination—a place of vision.

For too long we have cycled through poverty, disease, famine, war, greed, domination, and waste. We see it and believe it to be true. But if we start with the belief state, how we want the world to be, we find ourselves in a place without boundaries or markers. It evokes the artist in us and offers us the opportunity to create a landscape of future possibilities.

Wayne Dyer was a writer and motivational speaker who said a good idea is one you hold onto and that you won't let go, but a great idea is one that holds onto you that won't let you go. This is a time for believing in great ideas.

May we align our energy and our hopes to strengthen our beliefs.

May we bring to consciousness our vision for change.

May our resolve be as steadfast as our breathing.

May we be supported in our quest.

May we start now.

# Photographs

When Helen and I were young parents, we took a one-day workshop sponsored by Marriage Encounter called Parents are Lovers. Most of the day was useful, but predictable. Near the end of the afternoon the leaders posed one final question. The question evoked such personal emotions that I can awaken those feelings even today. The leader asked, "If you consider that time with your children can be reflected as photographs, in twenty years, what will your children's photo album look like?" At that time our daughters were two and four and our album felt brand-new, almost unused.

Today I like to think our albums are full, but only our children can say for sure whether our view of history is a shared one, or even whether the photos we would choose to include are on their screen as family memories. These photos are precious to me, and I will share a few of them with you.

For many years we owned a home in Putnam County, New York that served as a weekend place of refuge for our family. In the early years of parenting, our daughters were too young to bring friends along, and the house was too small to entertain overnight guests. We had nobody to fall back on but ourselves. So many of the photos in my album are focused on life in the country that it almost seems that the rest of our time was a functional backdrop of school, work, and entertaining: not nearly as vivid or vibrant as our weekends away. In many respects we led a double life—our lives in a New York apartment building that felt draining and tense, and our lives in the country that felt rejuvenating and spacious.

Each season brought its own special activities. Winter sledding followed by hot chocolates. We had the longest, fastest, and twistiest sledding hill of all the lake families, and our little community shared in the racing, falling, and trudging of sledding. Summers filled themselves with swimming, barbecues, and walks. Fall leaf raking followed spring plantings. A montage of times and seasons, smells and shouts, tears and laughter, such a brief time together as a family, so precious and so filled with memories.

The photo album I am imagining had a page dedicated to Halloween. That first year in the country as Halloween was fast approaching, we decided to buy pumpkins from a nearby "pick your own" farm. Once we were in the field, both girls immediately asked us to carry what were certainly the largest pumpkins in the field to the front of the farm where produce was weighed. In that moment we created a tradition. You could keep what you could carry. The chosen pumpkin had to be carried by the one who found it. Rest stops along the way were permitted, but the carrying was the true test. Each year the pumpkins got larger and our daughters' capacity to carry more weight increased. We probably embraced this tradition for over ten years, with the pumpkins growing to mammoth sizes. Eventually we switched from weight as the biggest factor to standards based on shape, texture, and size.

Choosing and buying the pumpkins only reflected half the tradition. After we paid and packed the pumpkins in the car, we returned to the farm for hot cider and freshly baked donuts. Hardly a model of healthy eating, but a shared experience that was just as significant.

My next two experiences are solo events, quiet but vivid. My daughter Dana has been in love with horses from the age of five. She learned to ride, jump, practice dressage, muck out stalls, groom, and care for the well-being of these beautiful animals. For about six years Dana owned a horse named Sal, a brown Warmblood that was sixteen hands high and weighed about 1,200 pounds. When Dana was seventeen, she was hired as a counselor at a riding camp called Vershire in northern Vermont. Before the summer began, Dana needed to transport Sal from Westchester County, New York to the camp, a trip of several hours that started at dusk and ended at 2:00 am the following day. I offered to keep Dana company as she made her first long-distance transport with Sal in a trailer attached to her small truck.

Our speed never exceeded 40 miles per hour. We made frequent stops to check on Sal, even occasionally backing him out of the trailer so he could move about. I was over my head and out of my depth. I served no practical purpose, other than to support Dana in this experience and to marvel at her skill, patience, and strength. In the world of horses, it was clear that Dana was in charge and I was the observer and student. Even though we arrived in the middle of the night, work wasn't over until Sal's stall was filled with food, water, and fresh hay. At 3:30 am, we found some bunk beds and slept until dawn.

I felt enormous pride watching how accomplished Dana was in the world of horses. At that moment I also knew she was no longer a child, but a mature adult with transferable life skills. My parenting role was shrinking and I felt a profound sadness that the inevitable shift in roles had arrived too soon. *I have more to teach you,* I screamed inside, *I'm not ready to make this change.* But, ready or not, ready had arrived. We grabbed some breakfast, I said my goodbyes to Dana and Sal, and drove home. The experience is now embedded in my mind as a framed photograph.

My next images are a montage of experiences with Amy, maybe at age ten, centered around the building of a complicated doll house we had purchased some months before. We stole time before bedtime and some hours over the weekends to cut, paste, trim, and decorate our dream house. The building was secondary to the sharing of precious time with each other. Amy knew that and I, like an alcoholic on the wagon, occasionally slipped into someone who needed the finished product to be equal to my affection. I grew frustrated when my fingers were too fat to attach the doorknob or put hinges on the windows so they could open and close. I wanted the house to be perfect for her, and I felt clumsy with the pieces that required a level of dexterity beyond me. Amy, however, never lost sight of our shared goal. Her slender fingers took the hardware from me and, with surprising agility, completed what I could not attach.

You might think that our photograph would be the completed structure, but that is only one of the images for this venerable object. After Amy's interests moved to tennis, school, and dating, the doll house was neatly boxed up and stored in the basement of our different houses, unopened until one day when Amy and our six year-old granddaughter removed the protective crate in which it had been stored for almost thirty years. Natalia was mesmerized by the figures, furniture, and structure. The provenance of the dollhouse was of little interest to her, but of great personal interest to me and Amy. And that is the photograph I carry in the wallet of my mind.

The amygdala is the part of the brain that stores memories associated with human emotions, a veritable point-and-shoot camera with great storage capacity and long-term memory. Downloading can be tricky and clarity a challenge with age. Even if you're not interested in photography, the amygdala is everybody's second camera. It never goes out of date and records in real time as events are happening.

The brain also has its own Photoshop. The beauty of this capacity is that the image we take can be seen in many different ways by viewers. The final product is a mix of memory, imagination, and creativity, although anyone you ask about a picture will swear it has never been retouched or altered in any way.

I want to go back to Parents are Lovers day. I want to tell the organizers they're only teaching a small part of the syllabus. I have images of work, of my friends, those with whom I had arguments and those with whom I shared tender moments. My wife, my parents, my teachers, my students—I am fascinated by the jumble of pictures inside my head that trigger memories from my past and lay my history bare.

Not everyone is a parent—but we all have been parented, whether by our biological parents, relatives, friends, or institutions. It would be cowardly if I didn't reflect on recollections pasted into the photo album that my head carries around from childhood. There are vacation scenes, scenes from camp and college, snapshots of restaurants and theaters, rides in automobiles, images of neighbors, friends, and family gatherings, food-prep scenes, and memories of the comfort foods that emanated from our small kitchen.

Yet all these images tease out events, not emotions. I wanted more. I wanted the secret moments of joy, of intimacy, of outrageous love. I wanted to hear the laughter and music. What I possess is the best my parents could offer. It was better than the albums in their own memory banks, and reflected their struggles to survive the Great Depression and the horrors of World War II. For that commitment, I have only gratitude for their perseverance and love, and for the effort they made to fill my album to the limits of their capacity.

My wish is that my children's album becomes fatter than my own and is ringed with laughter and hugs. My prayer is that my granddaughter's album will be even more robust than the one created by her parents. To get the right photo takes more than a discerning eye; it takes intention and dedication and patience. When you mix those ingredients together, you may just fall in love with an image, and that image might just love you back.

# Sorrow

Lately, the subject of sorrow has been on my mind. It's not a place where I usually dwell, but given that I am now more than seventy, I believe no topic should be off limits, and some topics should be embraced with a priority label attached. When I am poking at the corners of sorrow I feel like I am lifting the lid of a cobra basket—you know what's inside but you don't know how the cobra will react when the constraints are removed.

There are many kinds of sorrow, and many emotions that sorrow evokes. In this reflection my attention is drawn to personal sorrow, the sorrow grounded in loss, the most intimate of all experiences and the most universal.

When I invoke the word *loss*, I mean something precious to us that has been taken away. The loss could relate to our family of origin or the family we've created. Some of my friendships have a seventy-year history, while others, constructed in less than a decade, feel just as vital. The most obvious form of loss is the emptiness created by death. Subtler forms of loss also occur when there is a drifting apart, an ennui that shifts a treasured relationship into a kinship grounded in tedium.

Each person in one of these constellations is part of

the databank that makes me who I am. Some confirm my childhood story, others my college or law school years. And on and on for seventy years of witnesses, collaborators, buddies, lovers, friends, and family. Whenever one of them disappears from my screen, I have lost a part of my history, the validation of who I was and who I am. The documentary of my life loses a dimension, and what remains is memory, a poor substitute for the color of living stories.

Our mind stores moments, the times when...the places where...the people who...the images that... wisps of sound and movement that enrich our lives. We are constantly manufacturing new stories, but there is a preciousness to those with history that show the barnacles and fissures of life. Each story can touch our sorrow with a range of emotions that simultaneously feel both sharp and mellow.

Sorrow is the price we pay for love. Loss is the event, but sorrow is the experience. No one experience is to be weighed or measured or judged. As Shakespeare said, "Let us not measure our sorrow by their worth for then it will have no end." Our sorrow engulfs us at the cellular level, crowding out all other emotions. Given such power, how do we negotiate with our cells to make room for all the space that sorrow needs without needing all the space there is?

Our stories arise from the life we lead. We can either allow our sorrow to fill the entirety of our cells or we can create new stories that live in cellular companionship with sorrow. There is room in our heart for joy. The challenge is not in finding space; it is in finding the key to open that space up.

The new stories that we create some day will be tomorrow's memory bank. The names will change, the relationships will be different, and even the communication will have a unique timbre. What keeps constant is us. We remain the common denominator.

One of the early losses I experienced was my dad's death. I was married in 1965 at a time when my dad had already been battling pain and disease for more than fifteen years. Even still, he came to the wedding, energized and smiling. Helen and I left the party at midnight, went to our hotel room, and took a morning flight to Jamaica for our honeymoon. It turns out that my dad was experiencing congestive heart failure, left the party some time later with my mother, and went directly to the hospital.

After that, three days a week, either in hospitals or at home, we visited him as his health deteriorated even further. For more than a decade my dad had coped with chronic neck and back pain. As the years rolled on, he succumbed to pills and injections that numbed and masked the pain's intensity. The cost of this relief was to spend days and nights in a perpetual fog, barely able to drive, barely able to work, and barely able to enjoy friends and family. It was a slow decline. He had been a strong man. The unrelenting pain wasted away his physical frame and his emotional connections to all of us, leaving only an urge to find relief in escalating quantities of drugs.

I hadn't known that sorrow could be filled with all the little deaths that occur before physical death brings finality. We lost count of the number of hospital stays, the nurses that held shifts at our apartment, the growing dependency on others to help with basic functions. Throughout this time I worked, I tried to build on Helen's and my marriage, and I tried to be a caring son. When he passed, the first emotion I felt was relief— relief that his suffering was over and relief that Helen and I could now start to create our own identity, free of hospitals, funeral homes, and cemeteries.

I thought that sorrow had crowded out all memories of how I saw my dad. It took years until the image of his suffering began to share space with recollections of my visiting his construction sites, our weekend travels to New Jersey, courageous driving lessons, math tutorials, temple politics, and his steadfast patience, love, and support. We'd listened together as the Lone Ranger and Tonto saved the West, and as professional wrestling proved that good guys always win. We'd played nightly rounds of checkers, but as good as I got, I could never beat my dad. Those images hadn't been lost; they had only been waiting to be invited in.

Those joyous moments have outlasted the antiseptic smell of hospitals and the agony of my dad's recurring pain. During the intervening years, I have become open to recalling the memories of better times as well as the pain that memory evokes. As the positive memories reappear, I find there is now room for joy. I have learned that being open to joy can ameliorate sorrow. Over the years I have cobbled together a check list that I use for joy. Like all good recipes, your personal preferences will enhance the flavor, and convert a generic dish into a signature offering.

Tell those you love that you love them.

Tell them again and again.

Occasionally, don't just tell them—show them.

Take nothing for granted.

Start now.

Admit mistakes.

Learn to apologize.

Respect differences.

Find stillness.

Stay interesting.

Love yourself.

Celebrate.

Say "yes" when the universe offers you a choice.

Find out what gives you joy—and practice it daily.

Storytellers are to be revered, for they keep our stories alive. You are a storyteller for other people's lives and vital to their well-being.

# Tender Moments

The other day I wrote a piece that was part of a compilation of memories being put together to celebrate a friend's seventieth birthday. I wasn't able to be present at the luncheon, so I tried to join as best I could by writing down my recollections of a friendship that had endured for more than half a century. Over the years we have been together at weddings and funerals, shared the pain and joy of birthing children, shepherding their growth from infant to adult, and then watching, praying, crying, hoping, listening, worrying, admiring, respecting, and loving how they cut a path through the underbrush to make a life out of the endless possibilities before them.

The evolution of those possibilities sometimes gets snared by life events we hadn't anticipated. We experience such events as illness, the lottery, the economy, the bad or good fortune of friends and family. Interruptions or opportunities? Sometimes both and often neither. But all serve as instructional tools. When those close to us are learning life lessons, we have a front-row seat from which we can learn vicariously, while still caring, watching, and even participating in the experiences of good friends and family. Nobody is immune from life's seminal moments. Nobody.

There is a phrase that says *experience is what you get when you don't get what you want.* The unstated comment is that experience is the second prize—a disappointment to be tolerated. I agree with the statement that experience is an outcome, but I don't accept that experience is second prize. I prefer to think of it as the gift that keeps on giving. As long as we stay present, experience holds the seeds of wisdom, and the value of wisdom is priceless.

Experience involves viewing an event in the very process of its creation. These events include images in great detail as well as panoramic reflections seen from great heights. Close-ups detail the moment, crowding out any extraneous element that threatens to diffuse what is essential. Viewed from afar, we realize that nothing is extraneous, that everything is tied together in harmonious patterns.

When you have been friends for fifty years, images from your history go in and out of focus as you think back on the circumstance in which different adventures occurred. We recall dogs barking, cars honking, rain falling, and umbrellas opening. In truth we have mixed them up in our memory to create a coherent tale. What remains reliable is the composite feelings and powerful emotions that are the product of a continuing history.

We often recall the events in our lives as air-brushed, glossed-up and Photoshopped versions of the events as they unfolded in real time. We would swear we have not retouched the images in any way—and we would be wrong. Memories can be kind or cruel, unreliable as to facts, but prescient as to feelings. And feelings are the touchstones that tie us to each other. One of my most tender family moments involved my mother's passing.

My mother was a strong woman with clear beliefs about how things should be done. Her rules and lessons shaped my growing-up years and were tested by our interactions after my dad's passing. In many ways I was forged by how she lived, but my memory of her has endured because of how she died.

My mother's last trip to the hospital involved surgery for colon cancer. She came through that experience remarkably well for an eighty-five year old woman, except that her blood circulated poorly to the extremities of her left foot. A second surgery failed to alter that medical condition, and the doctor recommended that her left foot be amputated. She declined, and declined again, and declined once more, as a team of surgeons tried without success to change her mind. It wasn't just vanity; she had an utter abhorrence of being dependent on others.

My mother feared death, yet her decision to refuse surgery ended in death within a few days. The day before she passed, we shared a remarkable communication. She was calm, lucid, peaceful. "You know," she said, "last night Dave and Murray visited me and said they were waiting for me." Dave was her dead husband and Murray her brother. She was going home to be with family. She had experienced the ineffable—and the ineffable had been real. She died with dignity, with my love for her strength, for her glimpse beyond the veil, and for the gift she had bestowed upon us both as we waited for her breath to cease and her reunion to begin.

That word, those nights, our recollections, frame the tender moments of life. Our vulnerability has been woven into a kevlar fabric, making it impregnable, malleable, and unique. Wherever you are, start dancing. Capture steps, listen to music, nurture tender moments. When you read Mary Oliver's poem "The Summer Day," and she asks, "Tell me what is it you plan to do with your one wild and precious life," how will you answer? Answer with the truth. You are harvesting tender moments. And that will be enough.

# Turnaround

True believers say that *God doesn't close one door unless he opens another.* Doubters may agree, but will point out that *It's still hell in the hallways.* That's how change can feel as we travel into unfamiliar territory. The breadth of emotions we undergo can range from slight discomfort at one end of the spectrum to terror at the other end. How we view change is not an intellectual event; it is a cellular response stored from childhood that will be heard.

Does that mean each time we experience change that our childhood fears are likely to overwhelm us and control our responses? Experiencing change as something new, and not as a replay of triggered responses, is easier when we move beyond our habitual approach and truly consider change as a valuable opportunity. What would the experience be like if we could turn our hypothesis on its head, the one that maintains that change needs to be *hell in the hallways."* Why not consider change to be an adventure, an opportunity for growth, a chance to use our skills in a new way? In short, make it a turnaround.

> Turn around and you're two, turn around and you're four, turn around and you're a young girl going out of my door.

Change happens. We can be dragged along or skip along. Going out of the door into an untrammeled world offers us experiences just waiting to be named, tasted, and appreciated. As we go through these experiences, we will no doubt be shaped and re-shaped by them.

Let me offer two turnaround stories.

Some years ago, I was traveling on a Sunday afternoon flight to Washington, D.C., for a meeting that evening. I had been roused from a quiet weekend and resented the intrusion. The plane was almost empty. The seat next to me was unoccupied. In the next seat over sat a man of middle years who appeared to be struggling to write poetry with the aid of a Russian-English dictionary. After some time, he tugged at my sleeve, and in broken English said, "Excuse, please. Can you help? In Russian no prepositions exist. What to put in, what to leave out, not clear. I due to deliver poem to group in U.S. Senate. My host Al Gore." Then he blushed and added shyly, "I sorry. I not tell you my name. Yevgeny Yevtushenko."

Russia's most celebrated poet was two seats away, and asking for my help to complete a poem he promised to deliver later that evening. We spent a wonderful half-hour editing Yevtushenko's poem and connecting through our experiences. After we landed, I never saw him again.

In that short ride, I had gone from being a victim,

summoned to a meeting I hadn't called and didn't want to attend, to elation at a unique life opportunity. The turnaround wasn't meeting Yevtushenko; it was the life lesson that saying yes when it's easier to say no holds the promise of enrichment. That's what Madison Avenue captured in its message to entice New Yorkers to play the Lottery when it coined the expression *Hey, you never know.*

As I write about turnarounds, my granddaughter Natalia is turning ten. She entered this world with a life-threatening condition, but today a small scar on her stomach is the only physical evidence of her travail. In the hospital's neo-natal unit we saw her strength and perseverance, wonderful qualities that will serve her well as she grows into adulthood. There are memories from infancy that will remain part of her, even though she may never recall the details, but which will influence how she navigates her way in the world. She is wary of doctors and invasive procedures.

Recently, a splinter embedded itself in the sole of Natalia's foot that needed to be removed. After two days of waiting to see if it would come to the surface and ease itself out (it didn't), three generations of women (grandma, mom, and granddaughter) went to the local ER so a doctor could do the extraction.

The ER doc saw that Natalia was anxious about the procedure and tried to alleviate her anxiety. When the splinter had been removed, the doctor came out to the waiting room to talk to Natalia. He said he understood just how concerned she had been. He knew, he said, because he himself had undergone ten surgeries before he was eighteen, and had been deeply afraid of doctors, nurses, and hospitals. Then, one day, a new thought entered his mind. All these people that he was so afraid of had just been trying to help. For the first time, he was able to see them in a different light. In fact, he'd been so overcome by their intentions that he vowed he would become a doctor so he could help others the same way he had been helped. As he left, he shared one more thought with Natalia. Because of her childhood experiences, she might just decide to be a doctor also. And then he was gone.

> Turn around and you're tiny, turn around and you're grown, turn around and you're a young wife with babes of your own.

The speed of light is nothing compared to the speed of insight. Billions of cells receiving a new message simultaneously. The turnaround has already happened—it's only our mind that needs time to catch up and name it.

*Hey, you never know.*

# Watching Charlie Rose

Most nights Helen and I turn on the television to watch an hour of Charlie Rose interviewing folks who are articulate and smart, occasionally funny, and always informed. He's having a good time, teasing out information and positions from his guests. Most of them have recently authored a book, and the interview is a way of increasing sales on the author's behalf—an acceptable price to pay for the entertainment received.

Will Rogers was right when he said that folks won't remember 90 percent of what you said in a talk two hours after it's finished—but they will remember forever how you made them feel. That works for the interviews Charlie Rose conducts as well. You can feel the vibrations when Charlie connects with a guest at a very intimate level, and the times when he's just soliciting information. On those few magical interviews when the viewer also gets swept up into a common space, it can be as little as a word or a gesture that suggests intimacy, reflects on values, or resonates with your own core beliefs that someone else has touched.

In those moments the chatter all around us goes silent, our senses are heightened, colors seem more vibrant and we are, for want of better phrasing, more open to the experience of being alive. We become aware of our interconnectedness to others and the ways in which our choices have an effect far beyond ourselves.

And then it's gone. A brief moment in which we felt something special, only to have it move beyond our reach and fade from view. What we experienced had the resiliency of a bubble, the permanence of a wind gust, and the fleeting beauty of a smile. We want the experience back—but aren't sure what led to its birth or caused its death. When it returns, the experience feels like reconnecting with an old friend. And when it leaves, it feels as though a core part of ourselves has shut down.

For most of us—and for most of our lives—we operate in the "doing state" of existence rather than in the "being state" of existence. In the "doing state," we are efficient, task-oriented, goal-specific, time-sensitive, structured, and grounded. In the "being state," we are vulnerable, aware of ourselves and our surroundings, timeless, curious, expansive, and loving.

The doing state, as you might imagine, generally involves multi-tasking, the act of doing several things at the same time. As an example, we can talk on the phone while we check our emails, make notes, or create lists. Unfortunately, we think we're being efficient and assume that the nanoseconds we save matter. In reality, we are not fully present for any of the activities we are performing, and find ourselves "disabled" from the activities in which we are engaged. It is an irony that we have to go away to learn to be here. Retreats offer us the opportunity to sit in silence with others, opening up the possibility that we can relate to a "we" status instead of functioning in a "me" environment.

Those of us who have spent time at the beach—either on the West or East coasts—have heard of a phenomenon called the green flash. Supposedly, when you are at the beach and watching a sunset, if the day is clear and no clouds shade the horizon, at the exact moment when the sun disappears at the horizon line you will see for a brief moment a spectacular green flash. If you haven't seen it, you think it's just an urban myth. If you have seen it, you never forget you have been witness to a special moment in nature. The green flash can't be willed into existence—just as Charlie Rose can't manufacture a melding of his energy with the energy of his guests.

We need to find our own personal green flashes—those special moments that only happen when the environment is right and we are ready. Being ready is harder than it seems. I retired from work at the end of 2015 and am still trying to catch the rhythm of this new world. I look over my shoulder and see the past receding quickly. When I turn the other way, I see a site under construction but no roadmap for rebuilding. I resist the urge to fill up my time with things. Instead, I want time to engage in things I value. Don't be deceived by the word "things." It's more than objects that garner my attention. It's also people, relationships, and interactions. Looking forward, I suspect there is a lot of stumbling in front of me. The wisdom in this experience is not to stumble less, but to appreciate that stumbling is an event from which the green flash, some day, just might emerge.

I've created some rules of the road. When I follow them, I feel more alive, more vibrant. When I ignore them, I am not acting out of integrity—but out of expediency. It is a way of learning, but one that comes with lots of scraped knees.

*Rules of the Road*

Do things that make a difference—to you and to others.

Exercise patience in performance and in results.

Random acts of kindness is not a tag line—it's a prescription.

Get involved—stay involved. Make connections—keep connections.

Read poetry, listen to music, spend time outdoors, walk.

Don't rush through life unless rushing will make a difference.

The heart of improvisational theatre is to make the other person a star. It works in entertainment and it works in life.

# Coda—Finding Truth

If you have traveled with me through these reflections, it is now my turn to rest a bit and turn the laboring oar over to you. I will feel blessed if you and I have connected through the words on these pages.

We live in challenging times in which our entire planet is at risk because of our actions and indeed because of our failure to act at all. If we commit to saving the planet, it will be, this time around, through *conscious* spirituality, not *accidental* spirituality. We need to understand how greed and short-term benefits hold sway, and how our current minds can shift so we are not left keening over the death of species and the degradation of Planet Earth.

In today's world, much of what we do and how we do it surpasses reason and borders on the edge of insanity. At one level we can be detached from what is going on and simply observe how others behave. At another level, we can be swept up by what is occurring and participate without discernment or challenge.

Whether we take the path of observation or the path of action, I believe our behavior is rooted in one of two truths; what we believe is either grounded in fact or based on faith. Even when we believe what we're told is true based on fact, we know that facts change. For many, it doesn't seem to matter that facts change. People still argue for what was true in the past, even when it is no longer valid. When we rely on faith, our belief often stems from a concern that the facts no longer support our position.

We discover that the grounds on which truth rests have shifted. Even so, the new truth is ignored as we resurrect the old truth because we find it comfortable to maintain. When needed, requests to "trust me" are trotted out as a reason to maintain a fallacious position. Trust becomes the paradigm that allows truth to shift its form without shifting its rationale.

Recognition precedes action, but does not replace it. We need to be bold enough that we challenge assumptions in light of new information, view matters through a skeptic's eye to recognize the difference between manipulation and modification, and embrace a skeptic's heart to challenge resistance. The more visible we become, the more resistance we will encounter.

When neither fact nor faith seems to withstand scrutiny, how do we create space for truly open inquiry, and then let it lead us to sustainable change? Survival is based on our determination to challenge both fact and faith, to lift rocks to see what's underneath, question infallibility, recognize and appreciate that threads of sanity exist in our collective craziness. If we adhere to these principles, humankind may flourish. Otherwise our sun shall become one of the billions of stars in the universe without a sustainable life form. And no one will be left to witness our dying or mourn our passing.

# The Author

George Kaufman is a writer, lawyer, storyteller and spiritual seeker. For many years he was closely affiliated with Omega, a holistic educational institute located near Rhinebeck, New York. During his association with Omega, George served as a board member, Vice-Chair and Chair of the Institute. He also directed their development department, which is responsible for that organization's fundraising activities. While practicing law in New York and Washington, D.C., he lectured for the Practicing Law Institute and wrote articles, columns, and a book published by the American Bar Association titled *The Lawyer's Guide to Balancing Life and Work*.

After a lifetime on the East Coast, George and his wife Helen moved in 2015 to Eugene, OR. Helen is an artist, therapist, his best friend and trusted ally. George has two children and a beautiful grandchild. In a world that is increasingly difficult to navigate, they are intrepid sailors.

Made in the USA
San Bernardino, CA
07 April 2018